MANDALA
COLORING BOOK DESIGNS

A CALMING AND CREATIVE ESCAPE FOR ADULTS AND CHILDREN

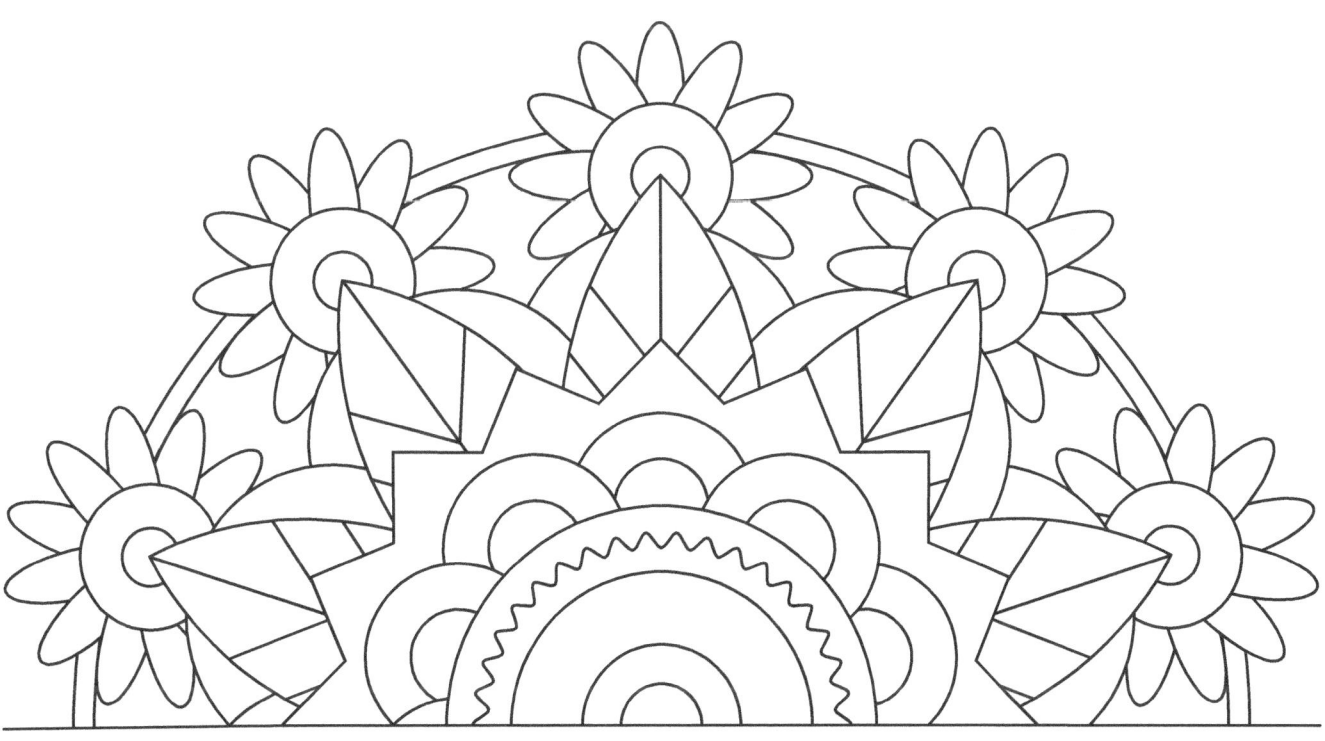

ENTERLINE DESIGN SERVICES LLC

ISBN 978-1-944750-00-8

Thanks for choosing this coloring book. We hope you enjoy coloring the 30 unique and creative mandala designs within these pages. With various levels of detail and difficulty, this book can be enjoyed by both young and older creatives. We hope these inspiring designs will bring a calming and enjoyable escape for you and your family.

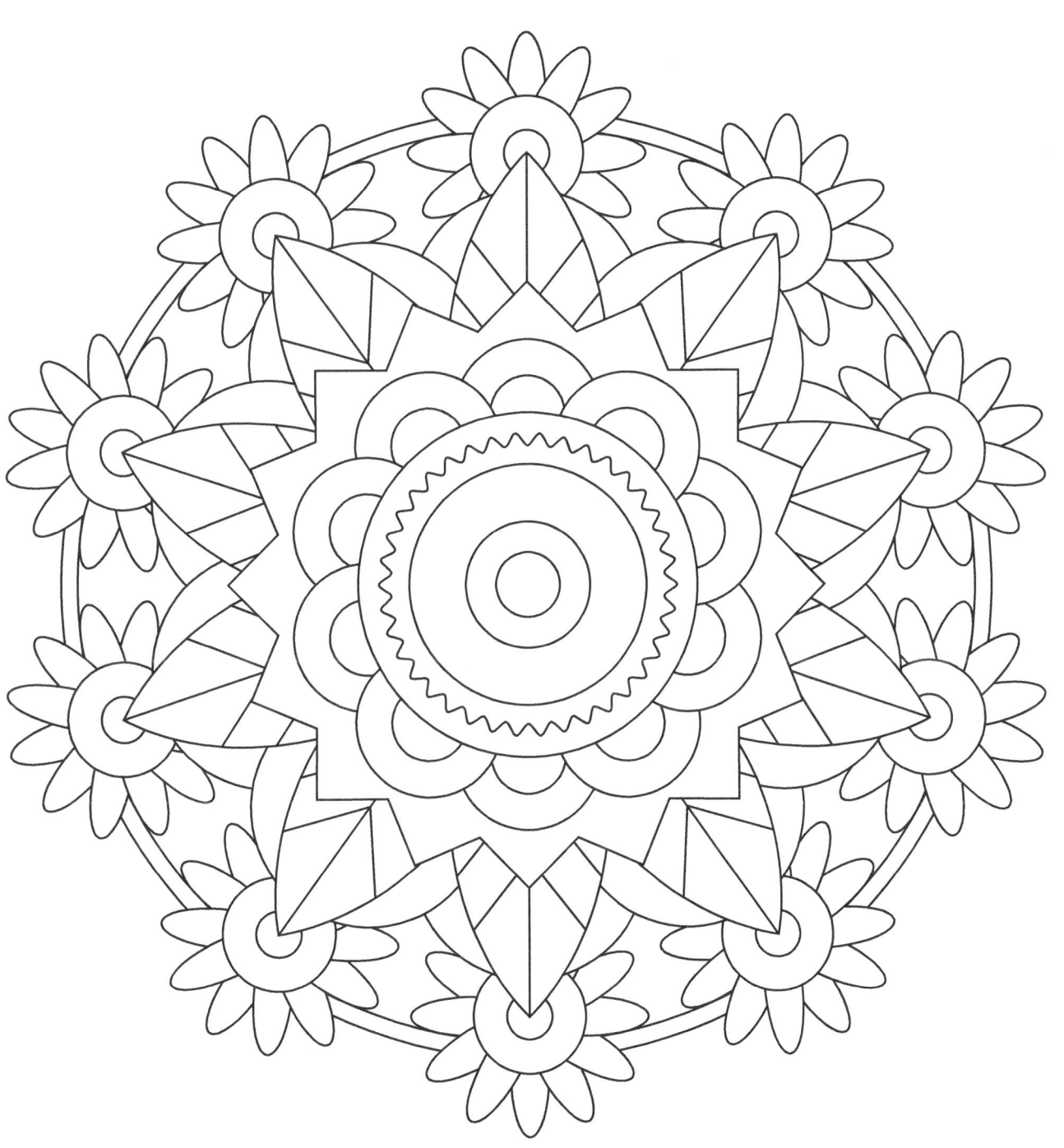

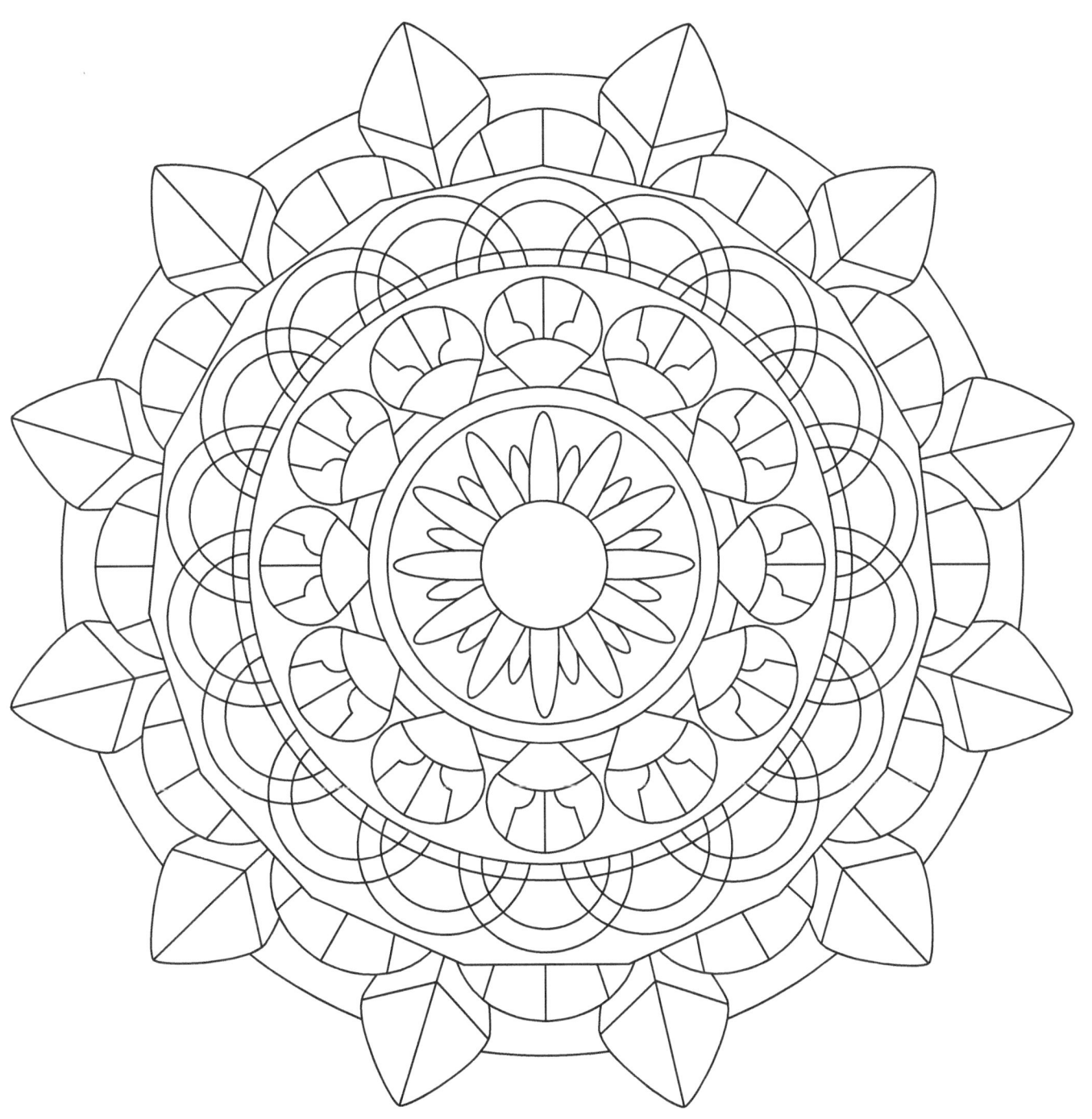

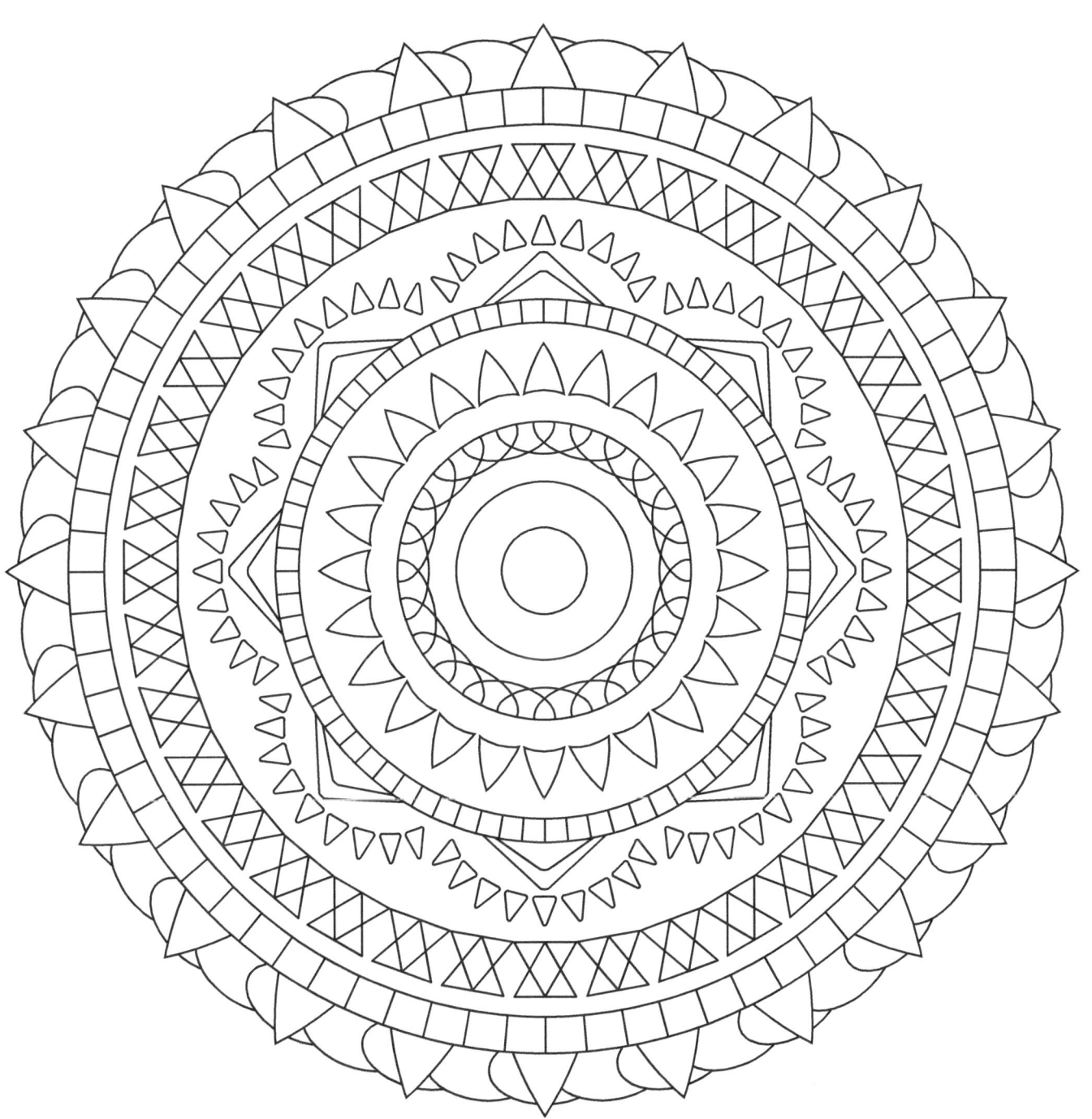

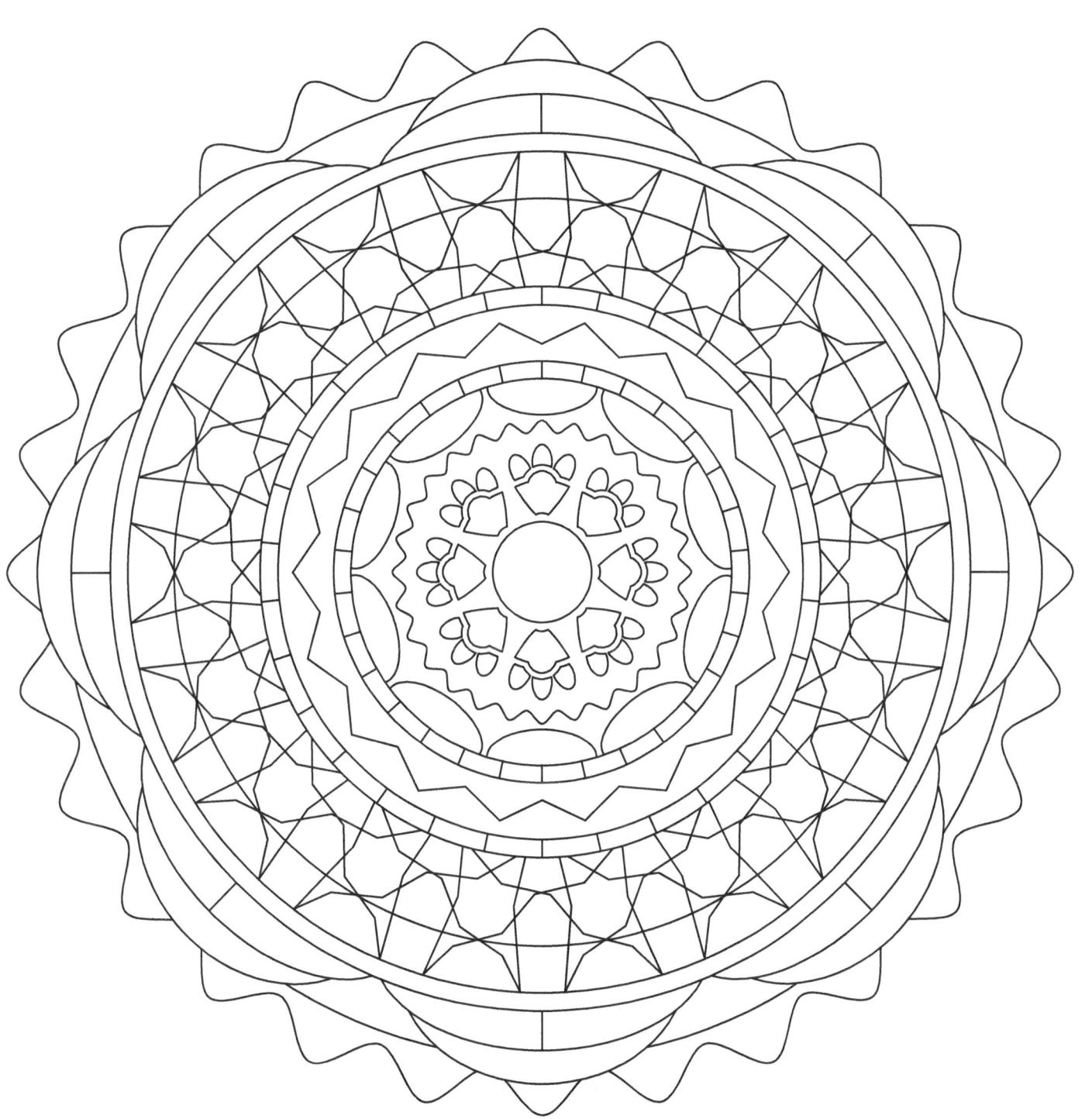

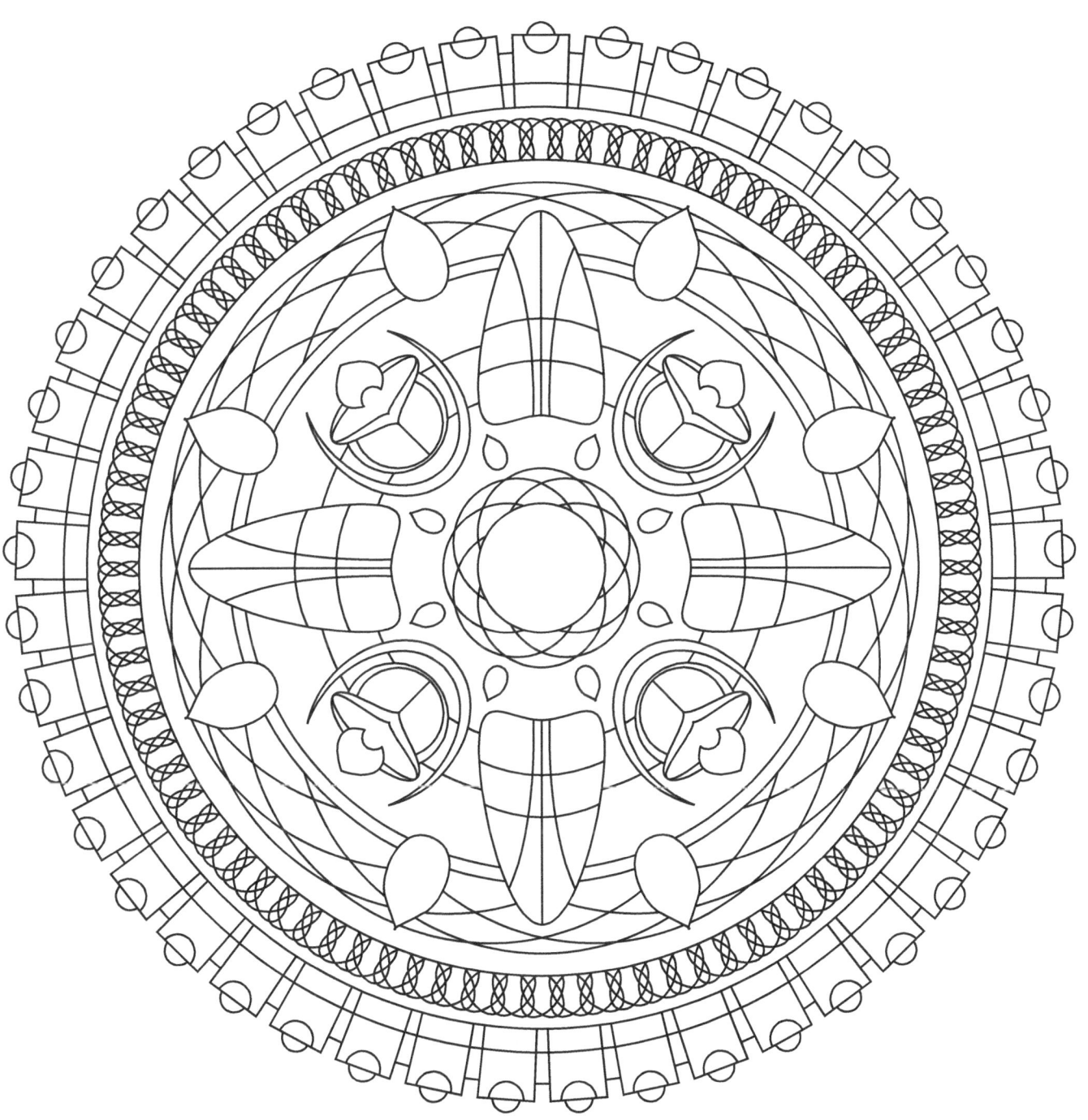

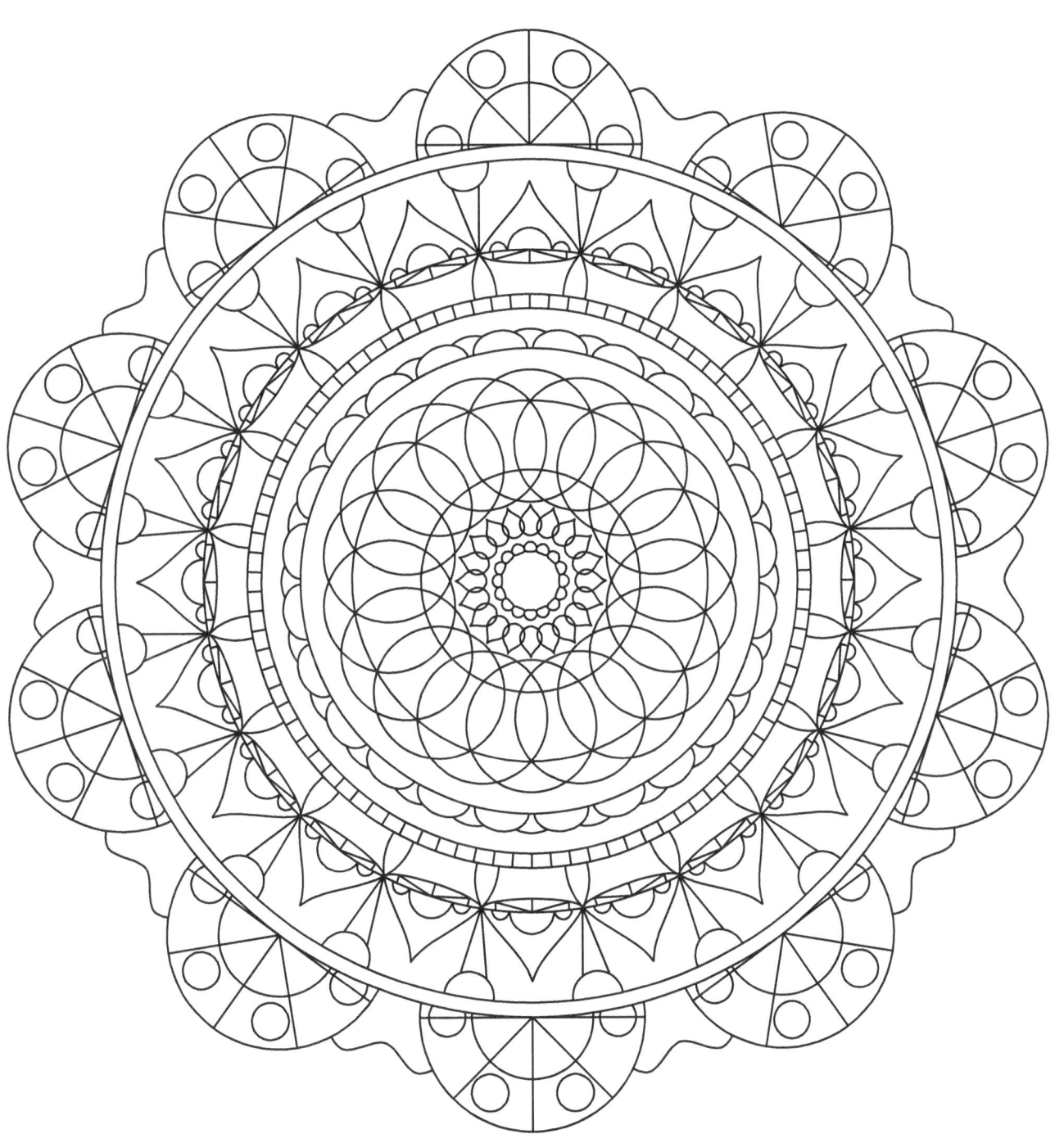

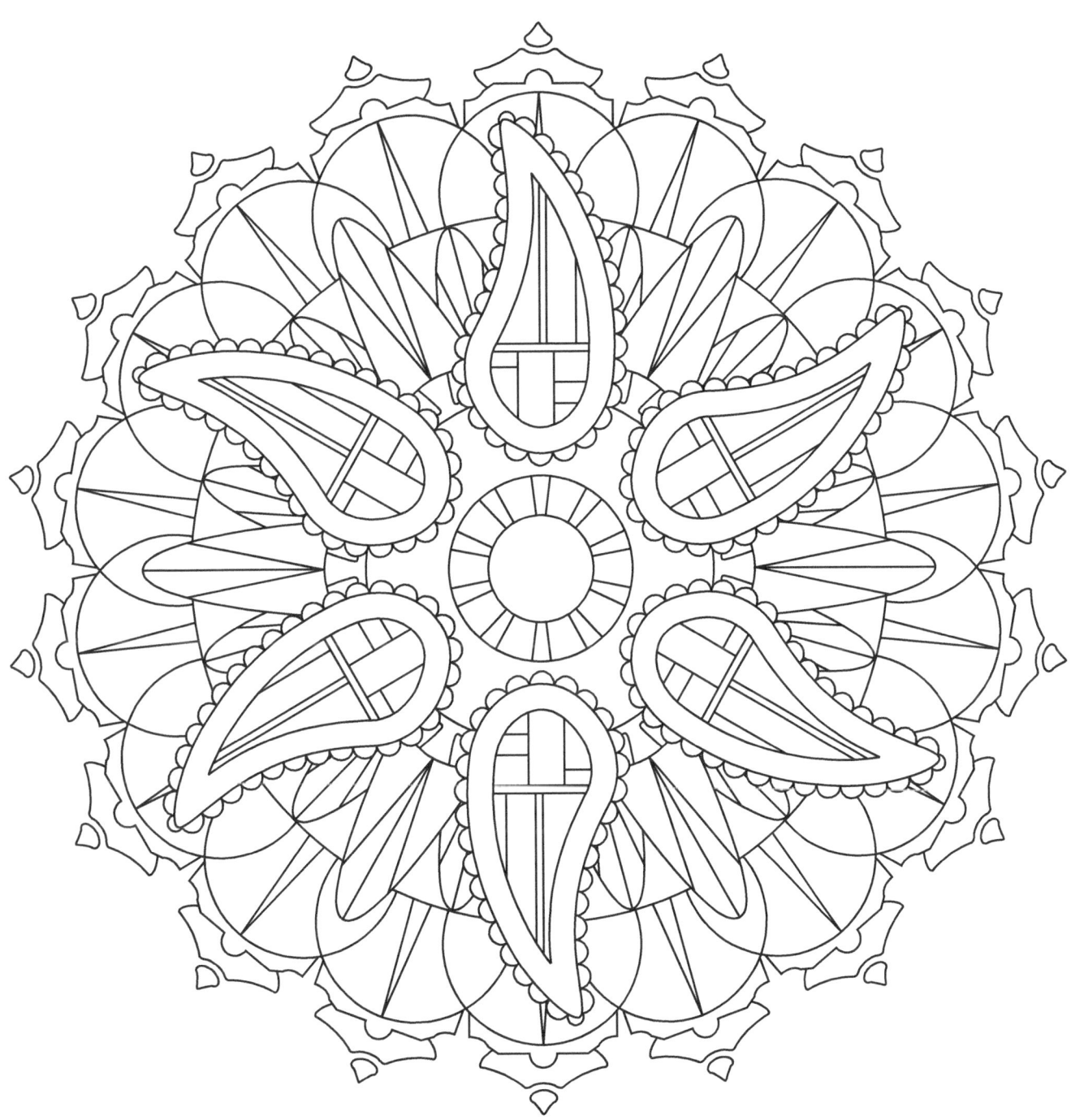

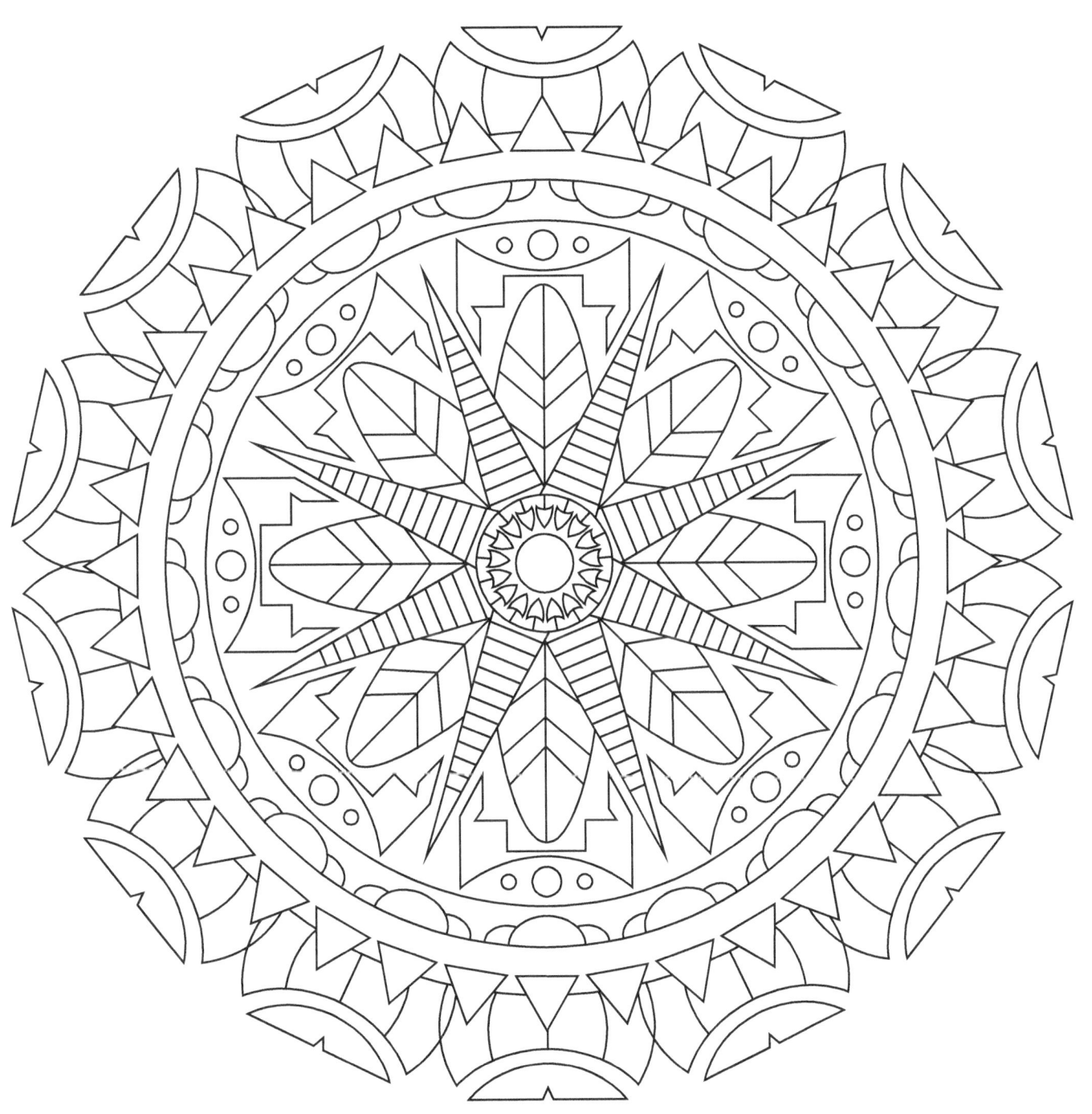

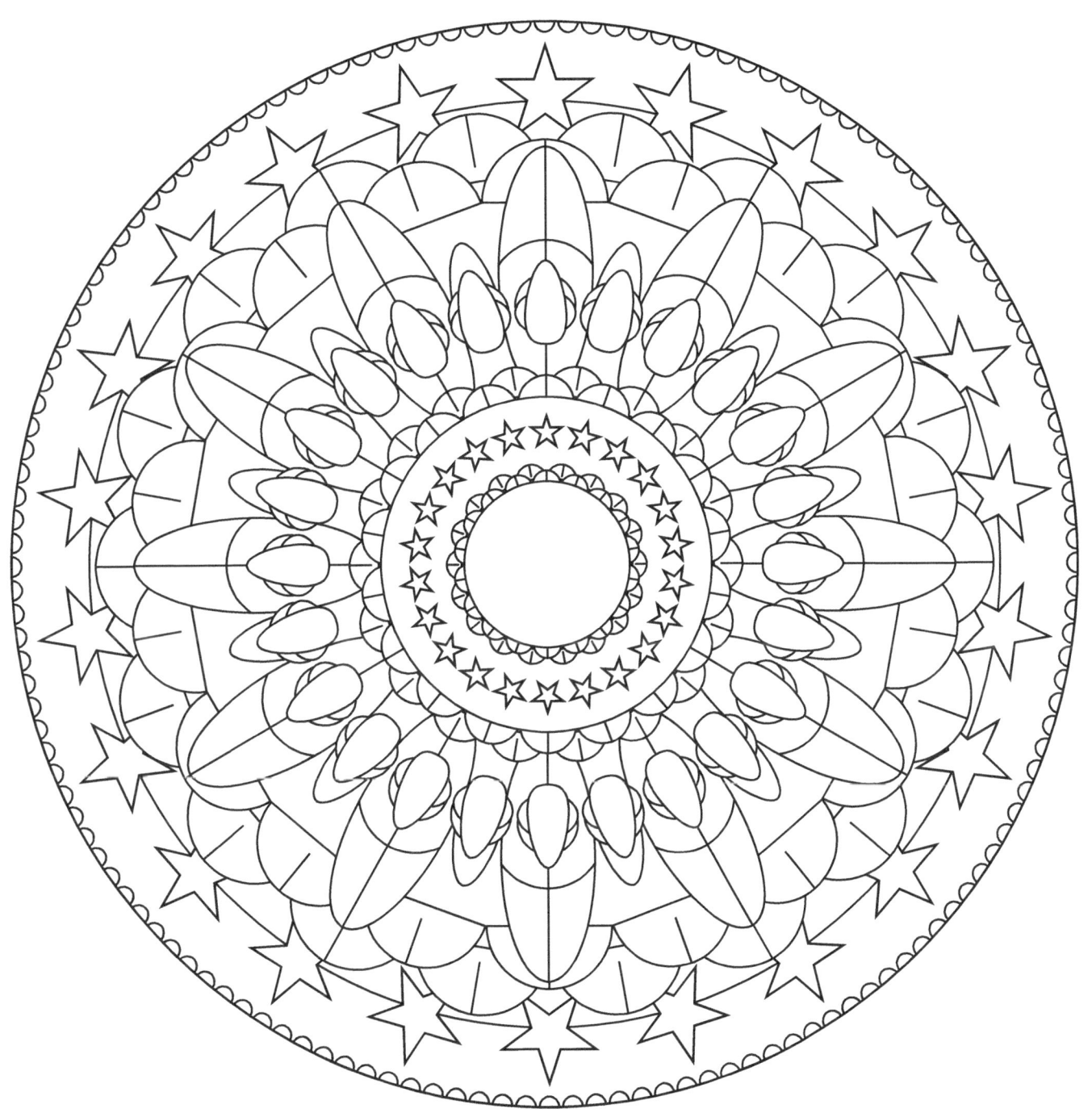

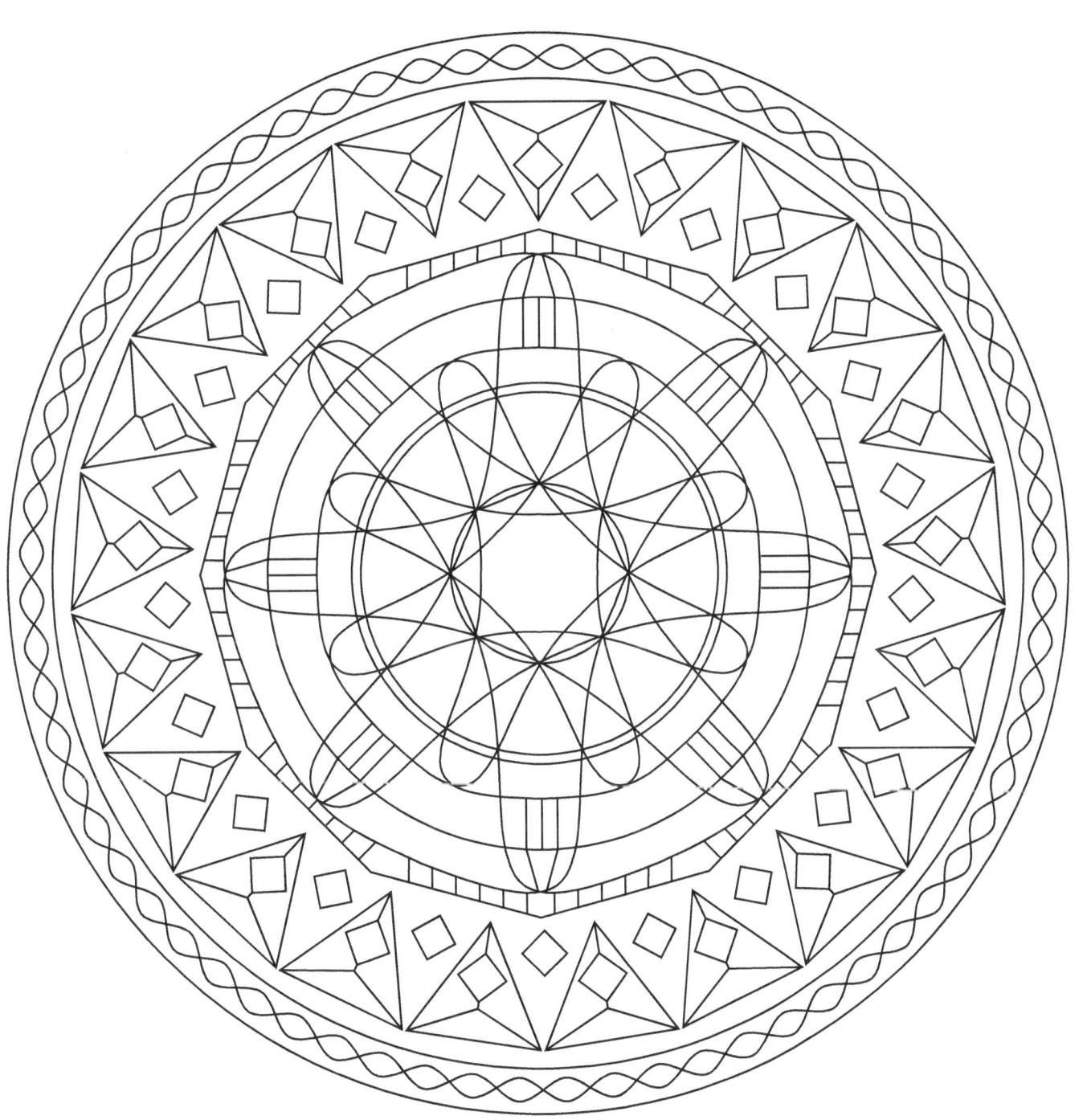

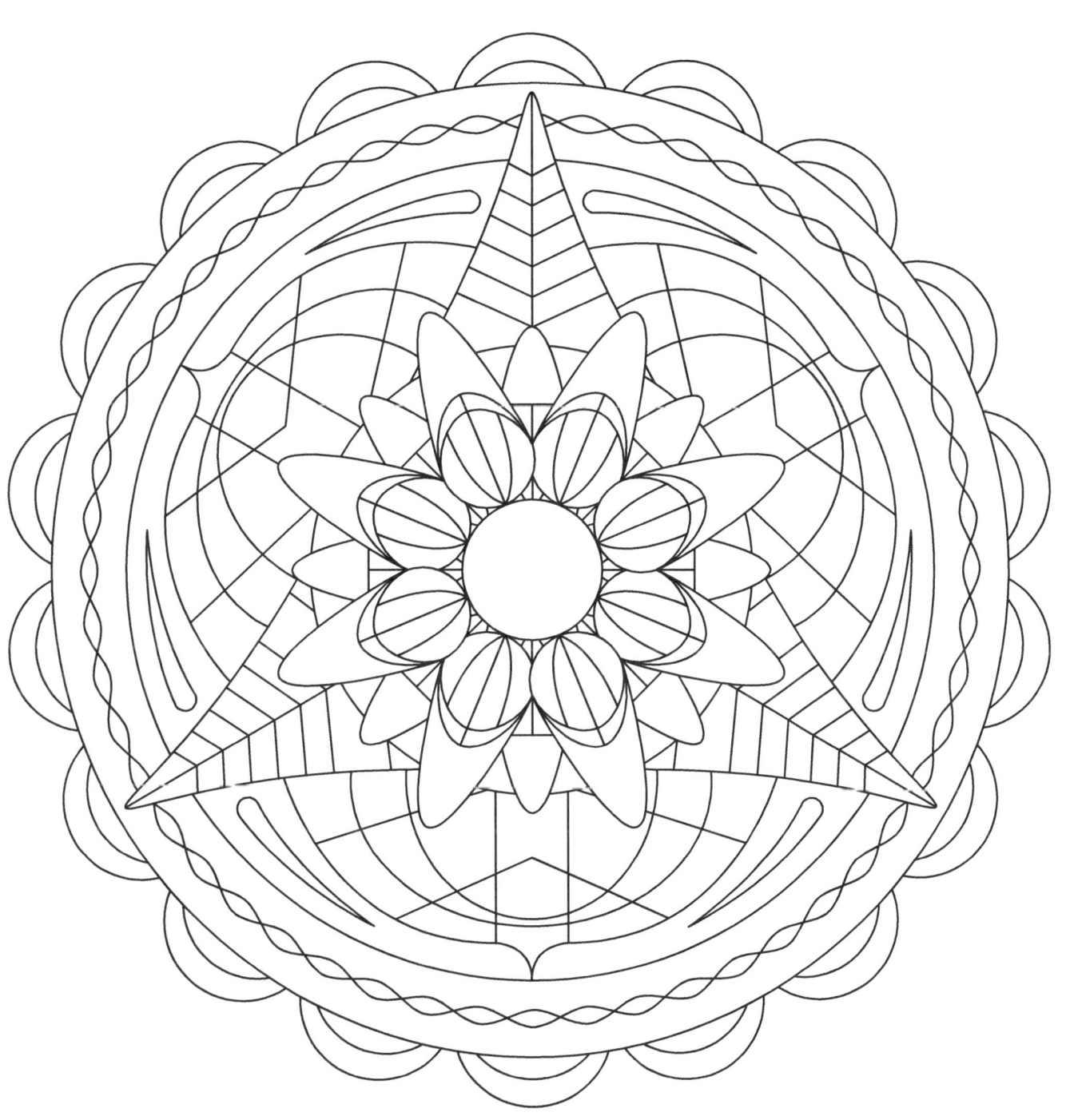

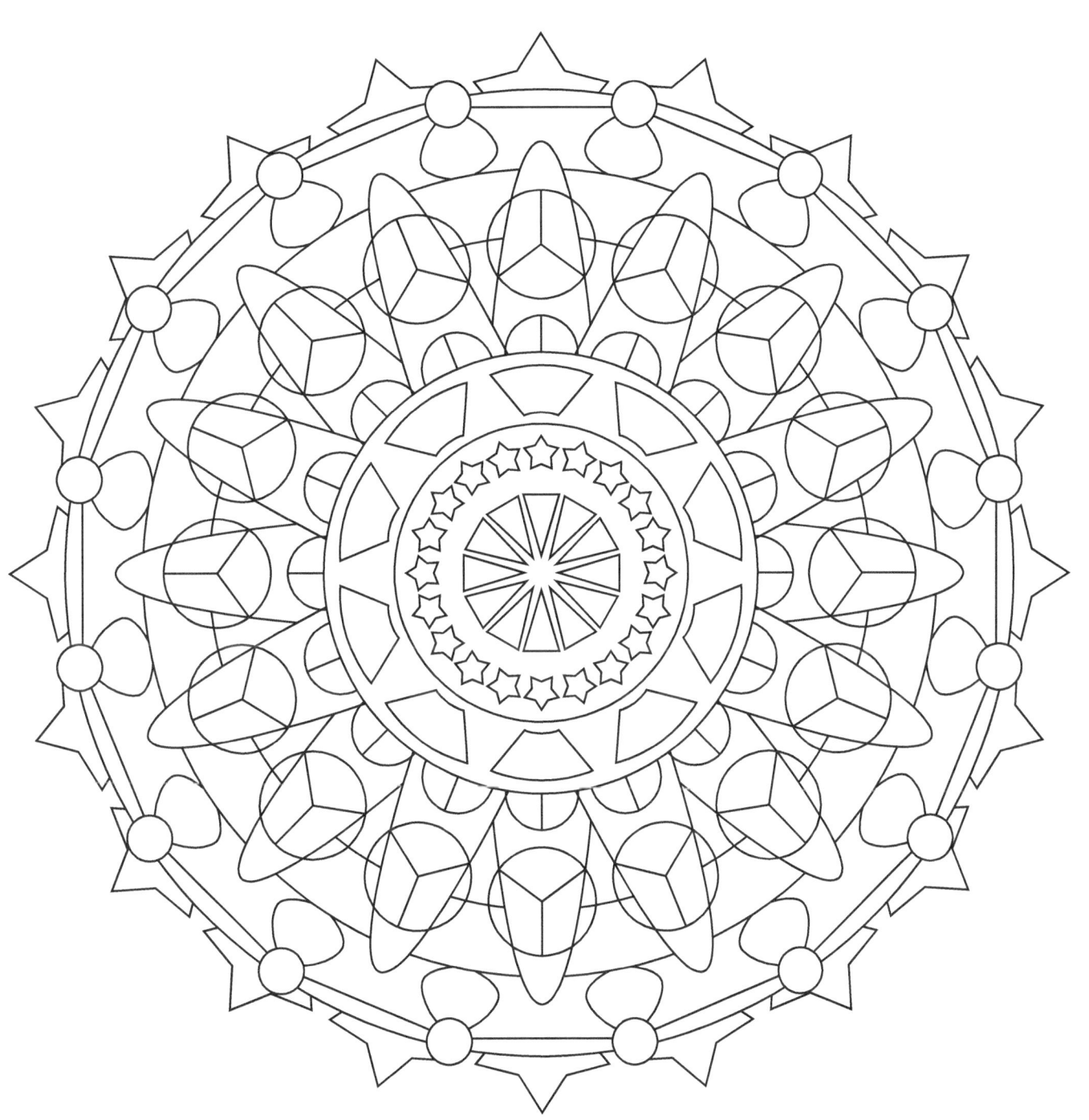

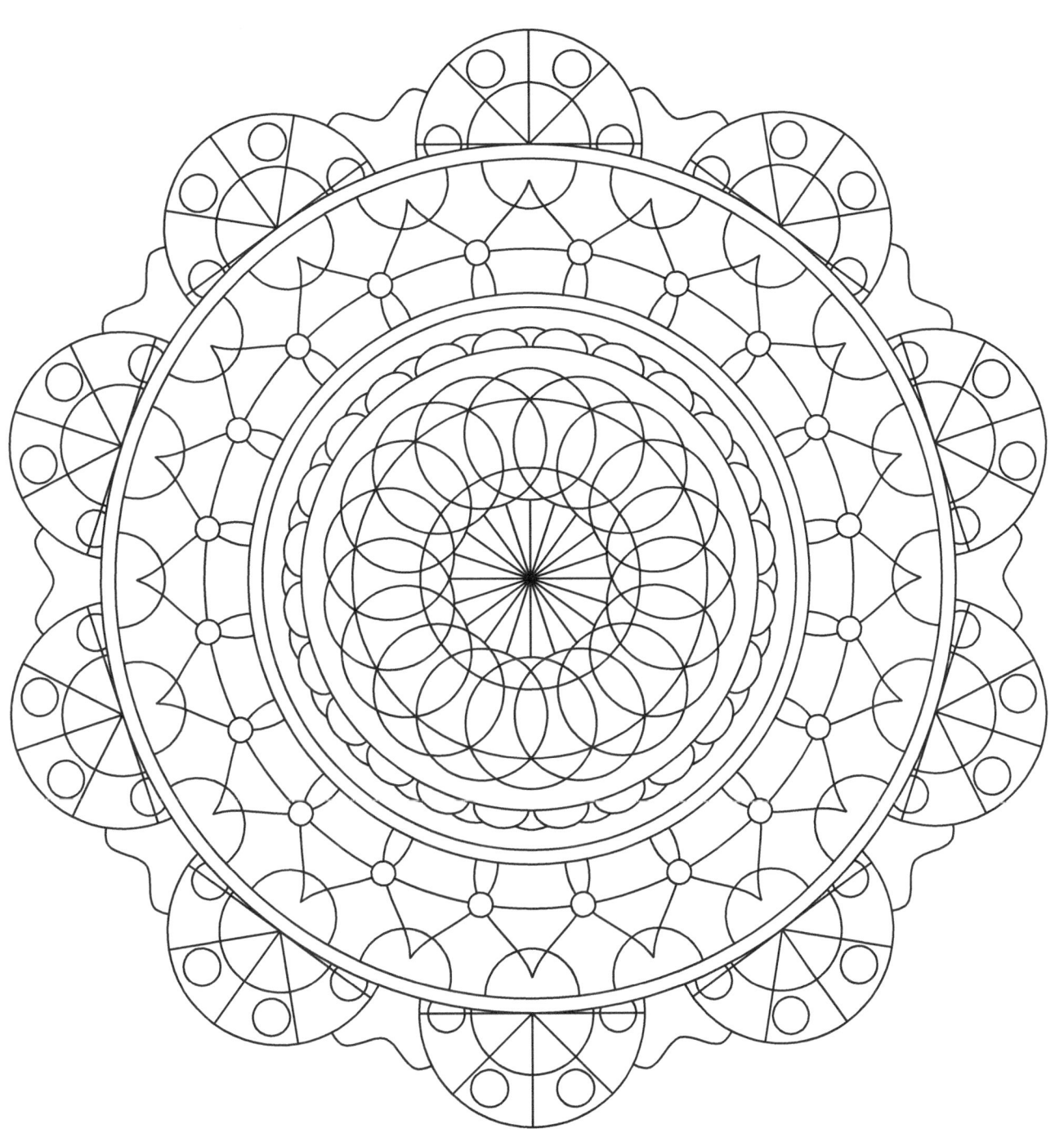

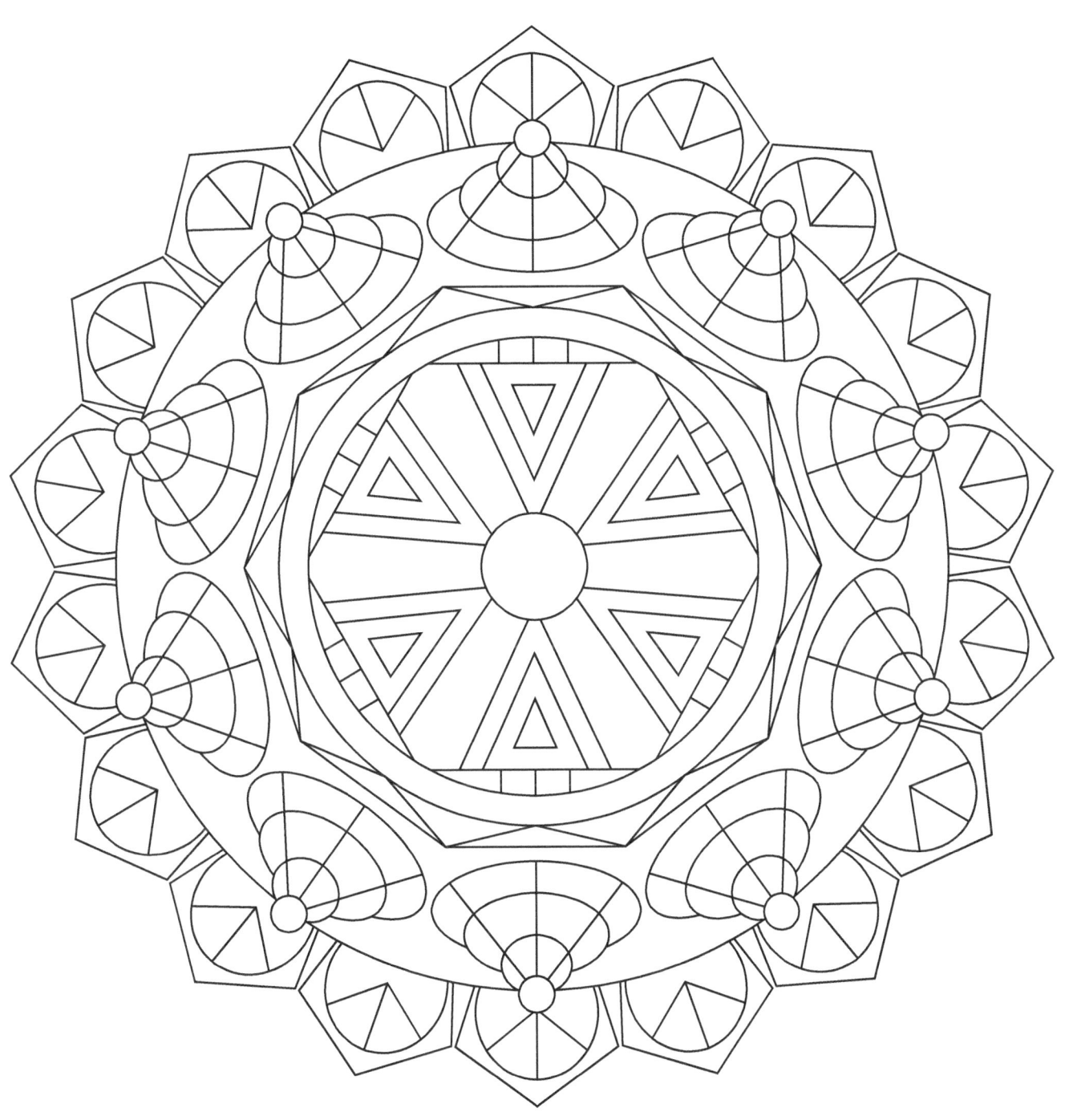

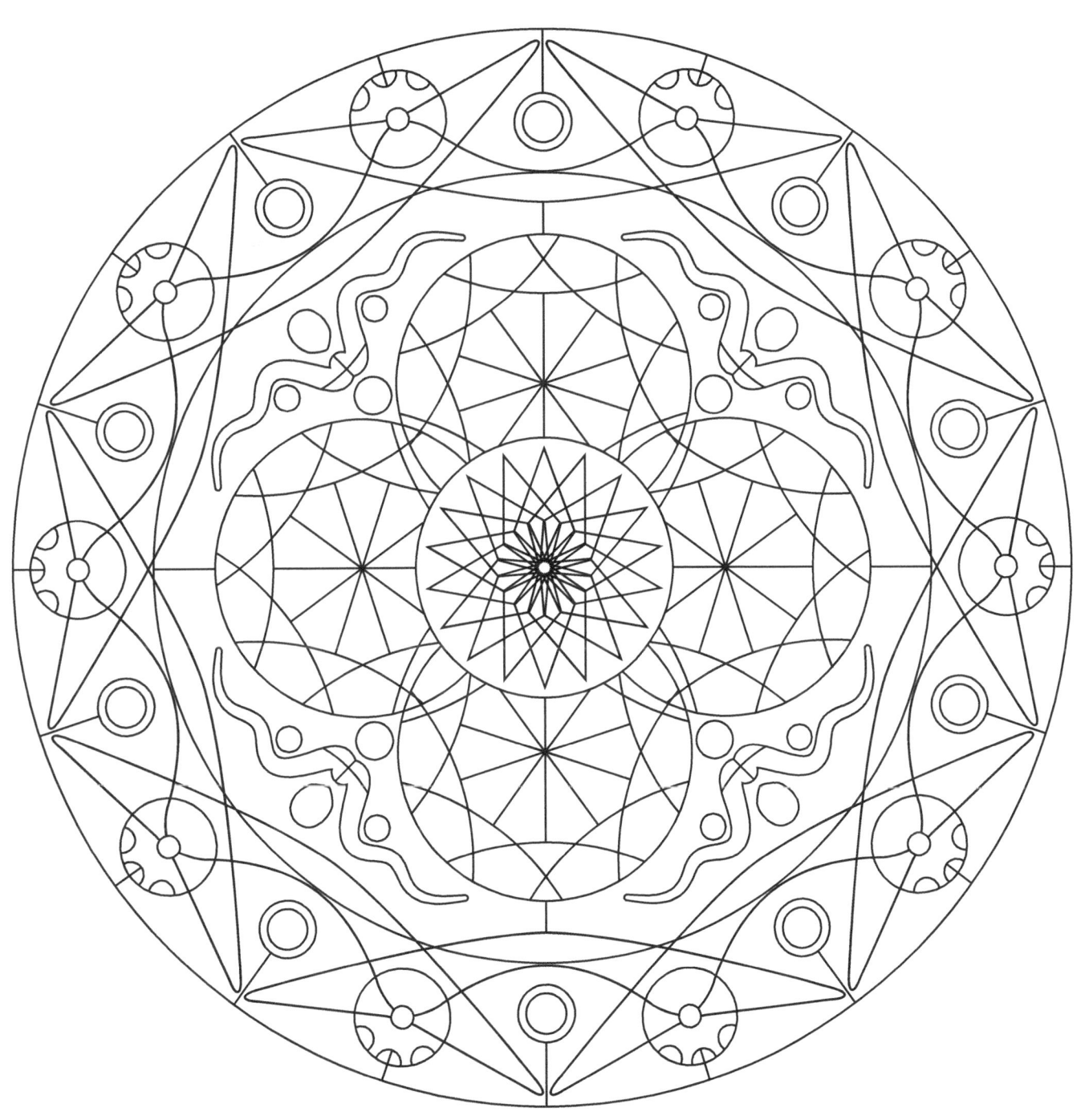

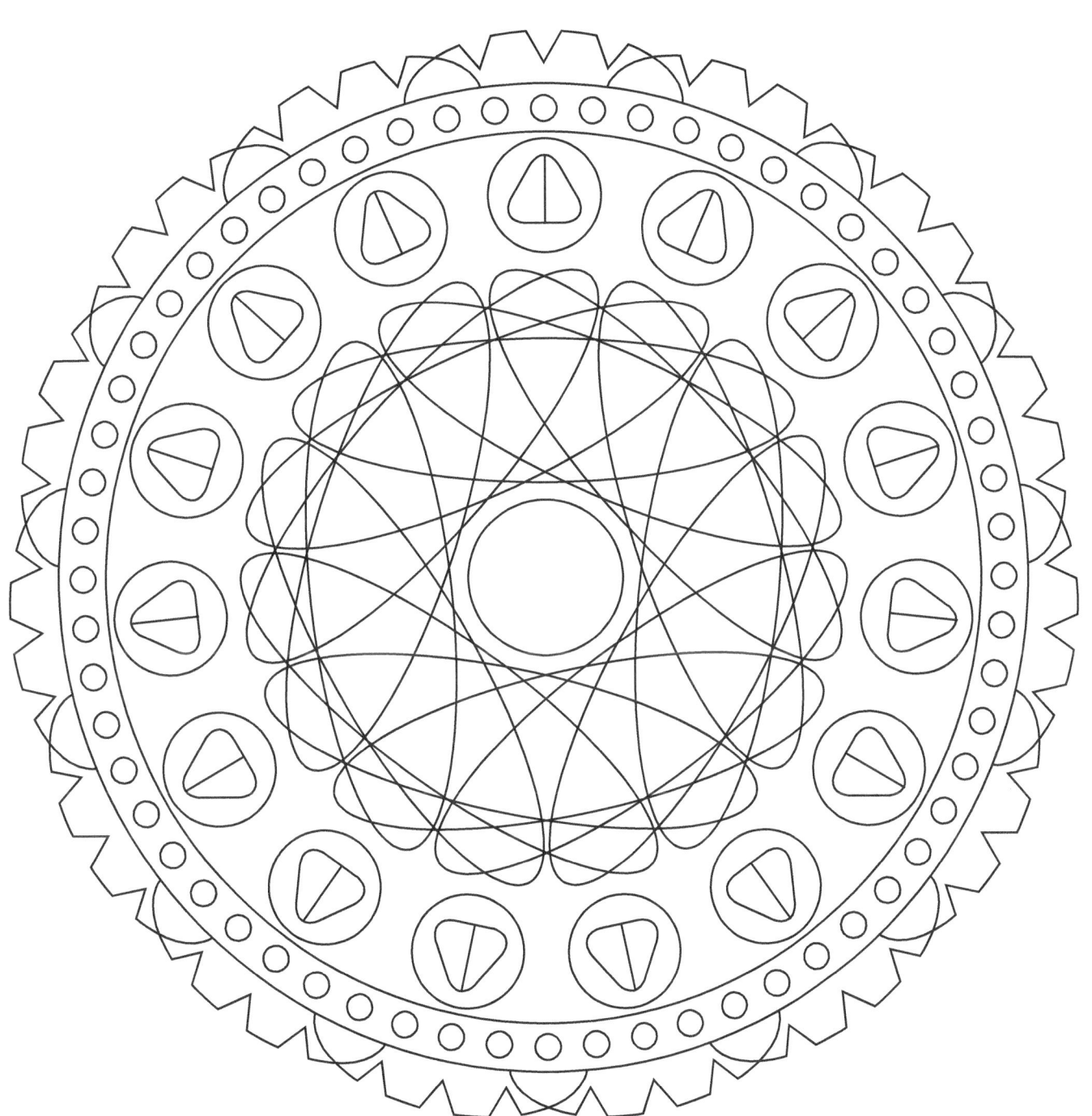

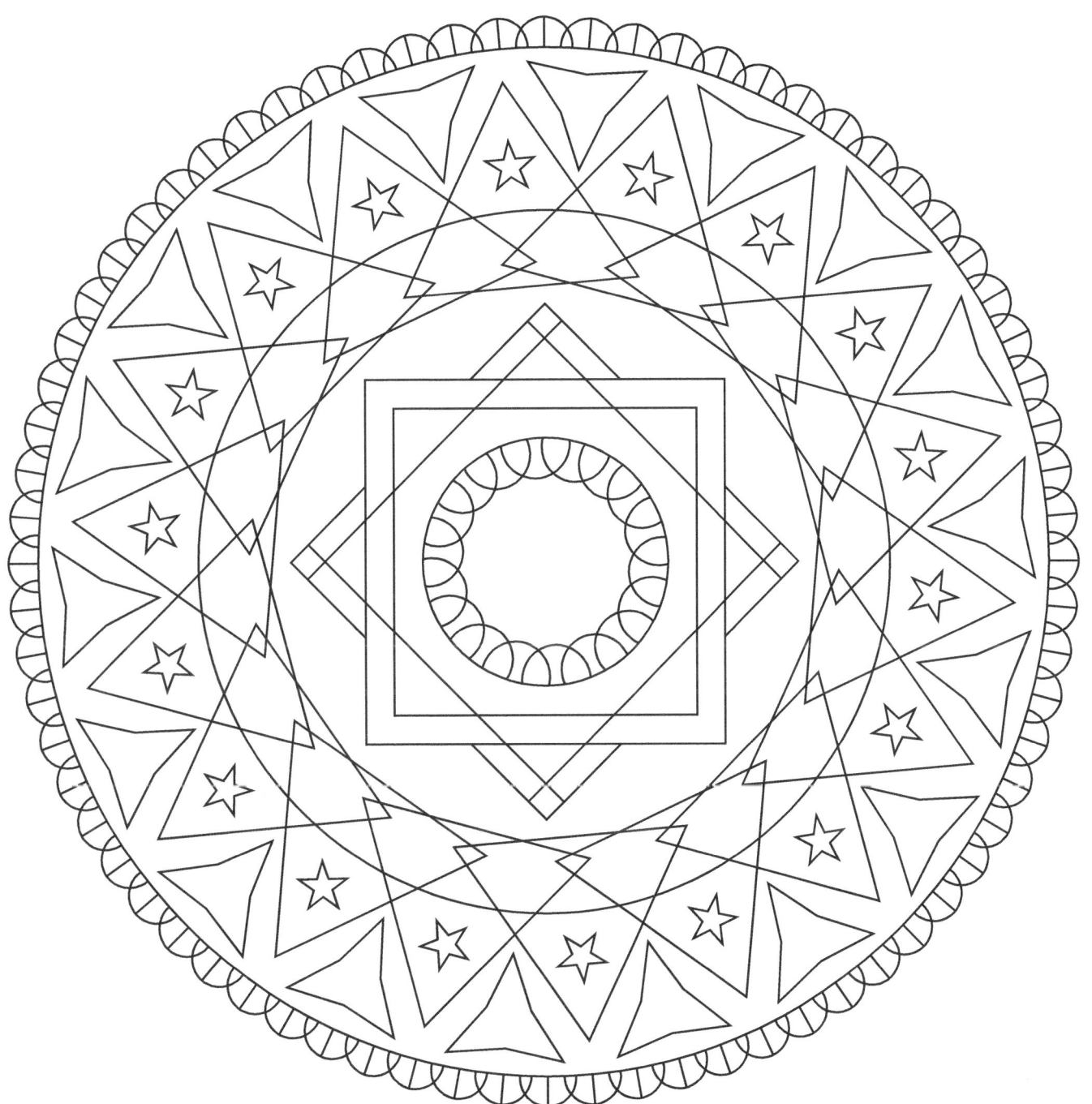

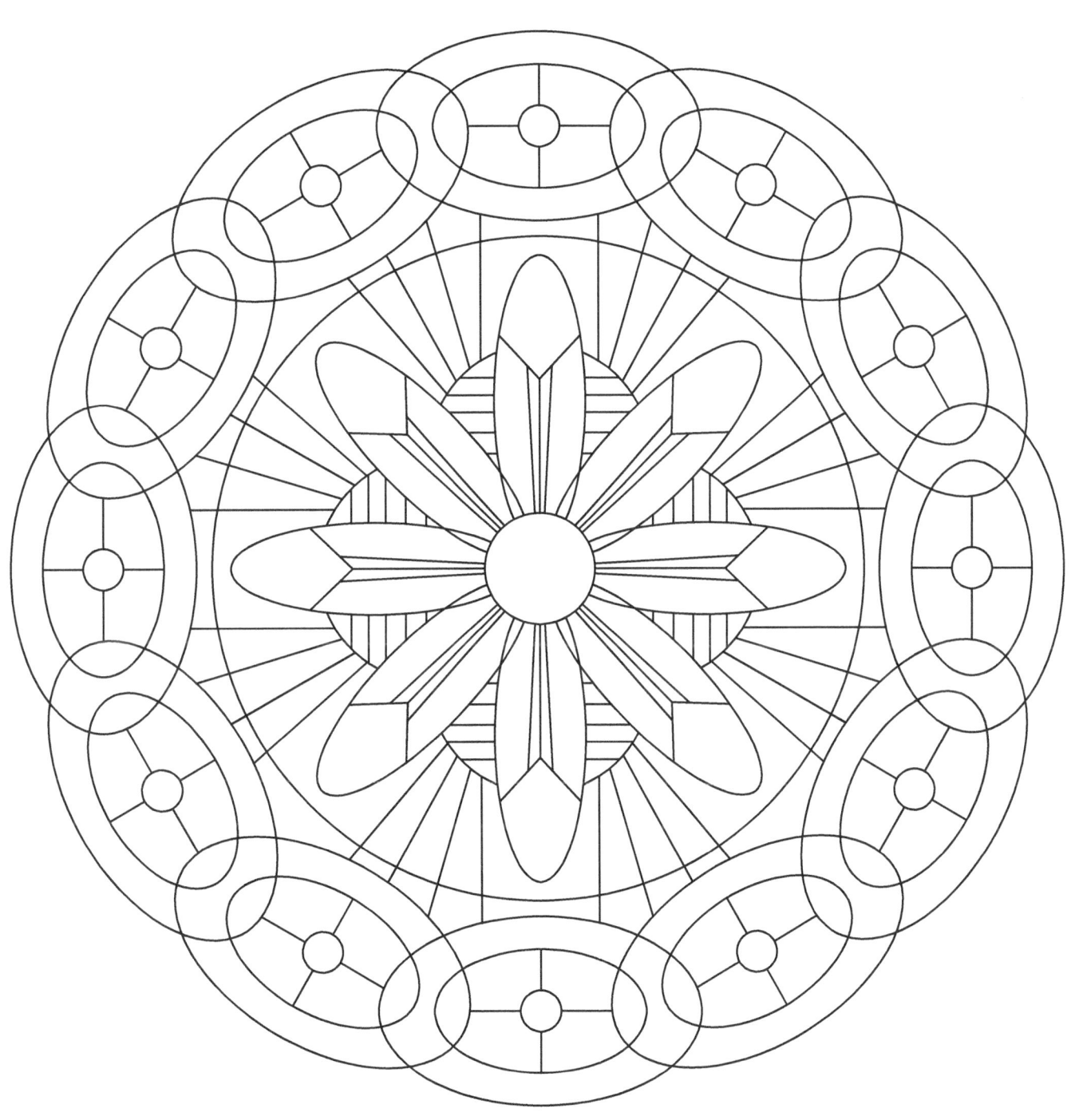

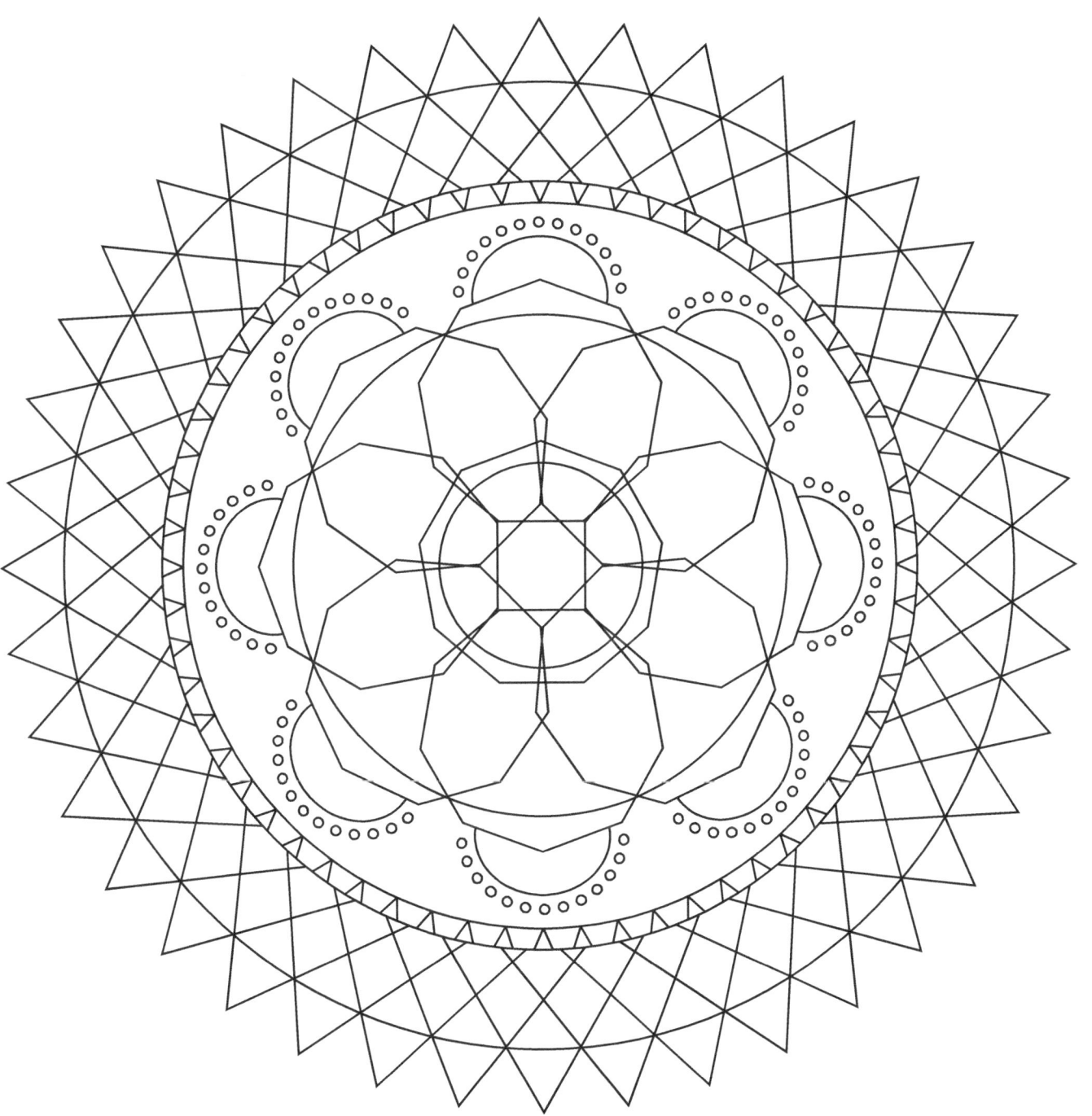

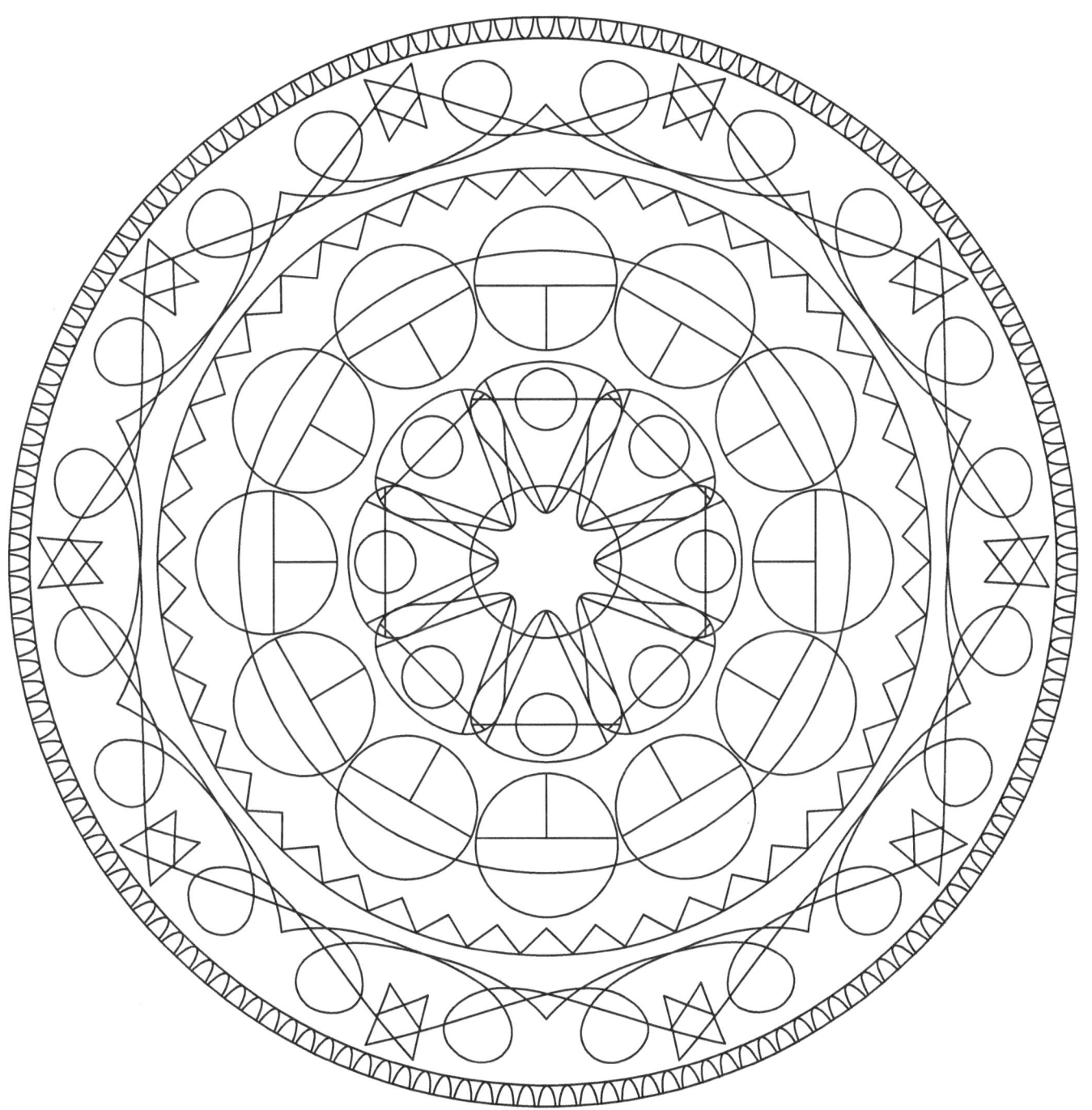

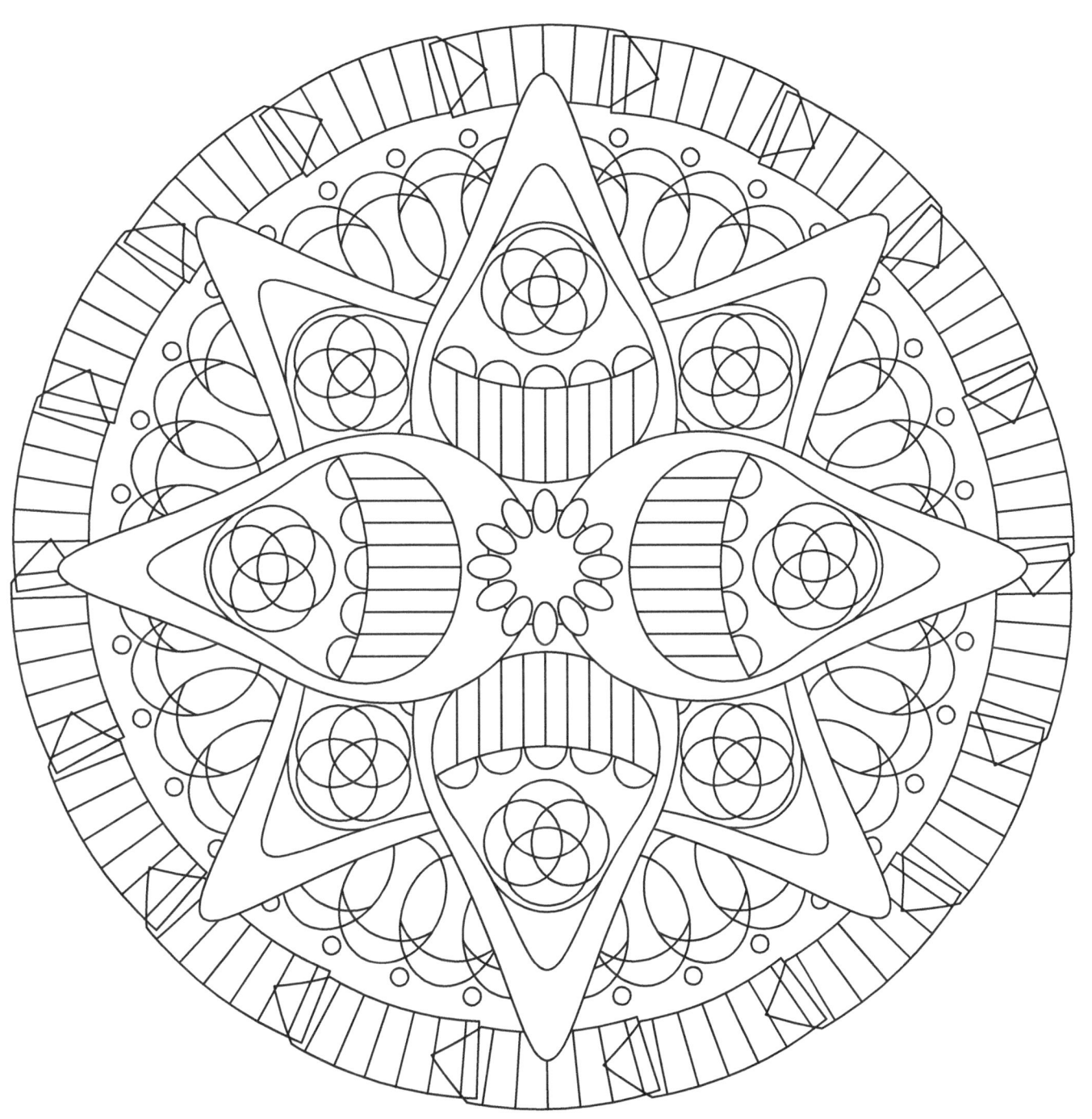

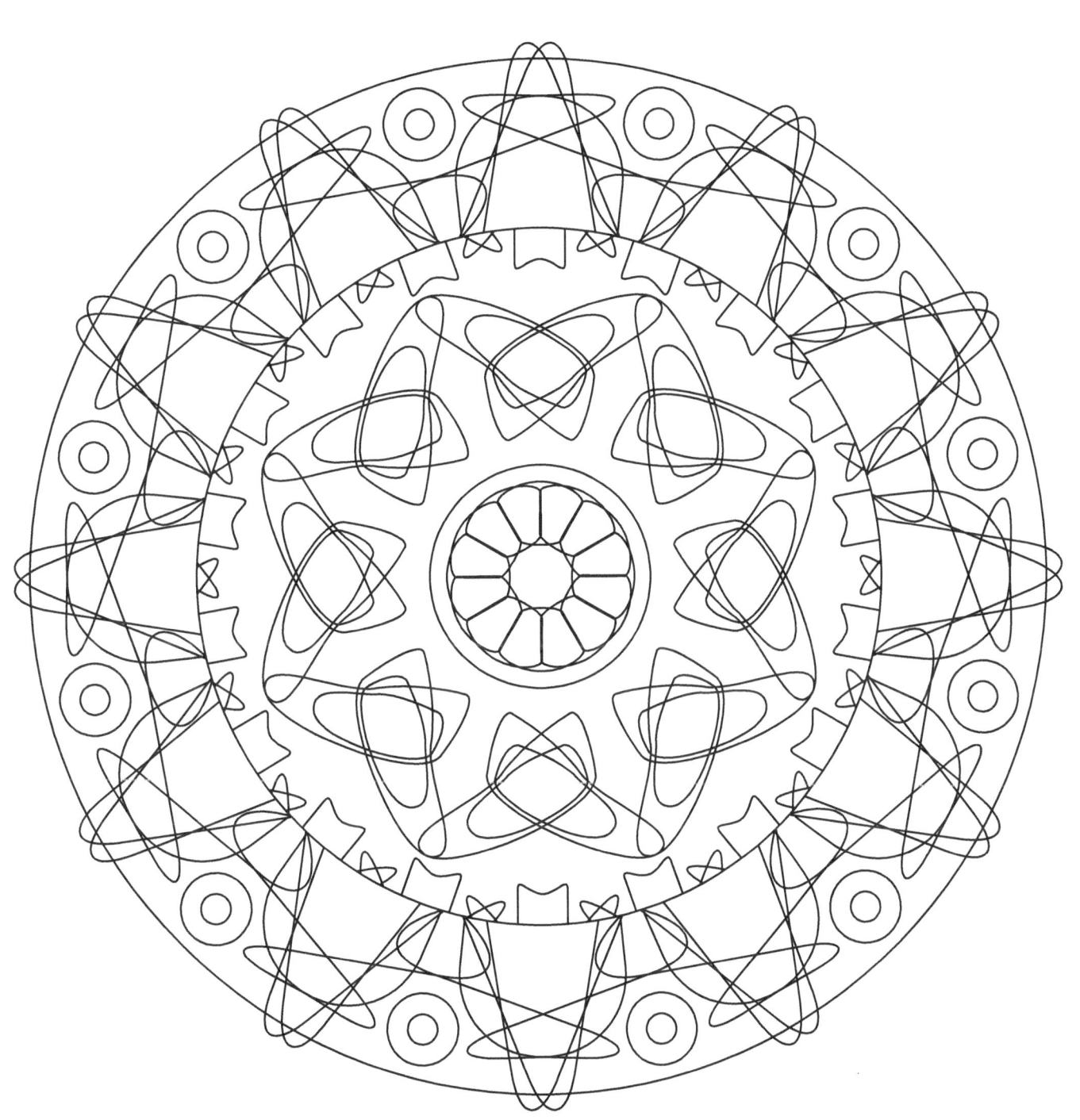

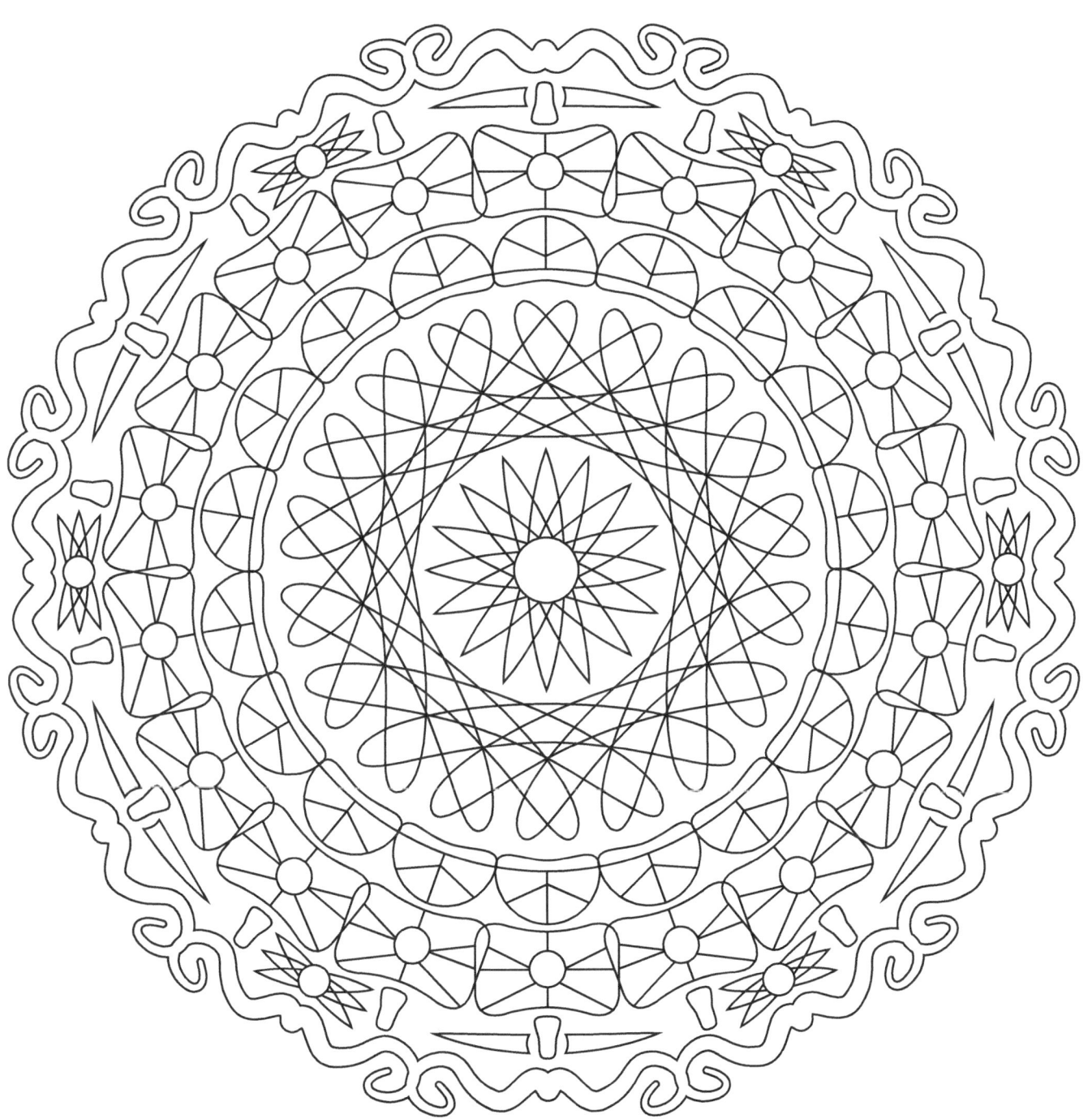

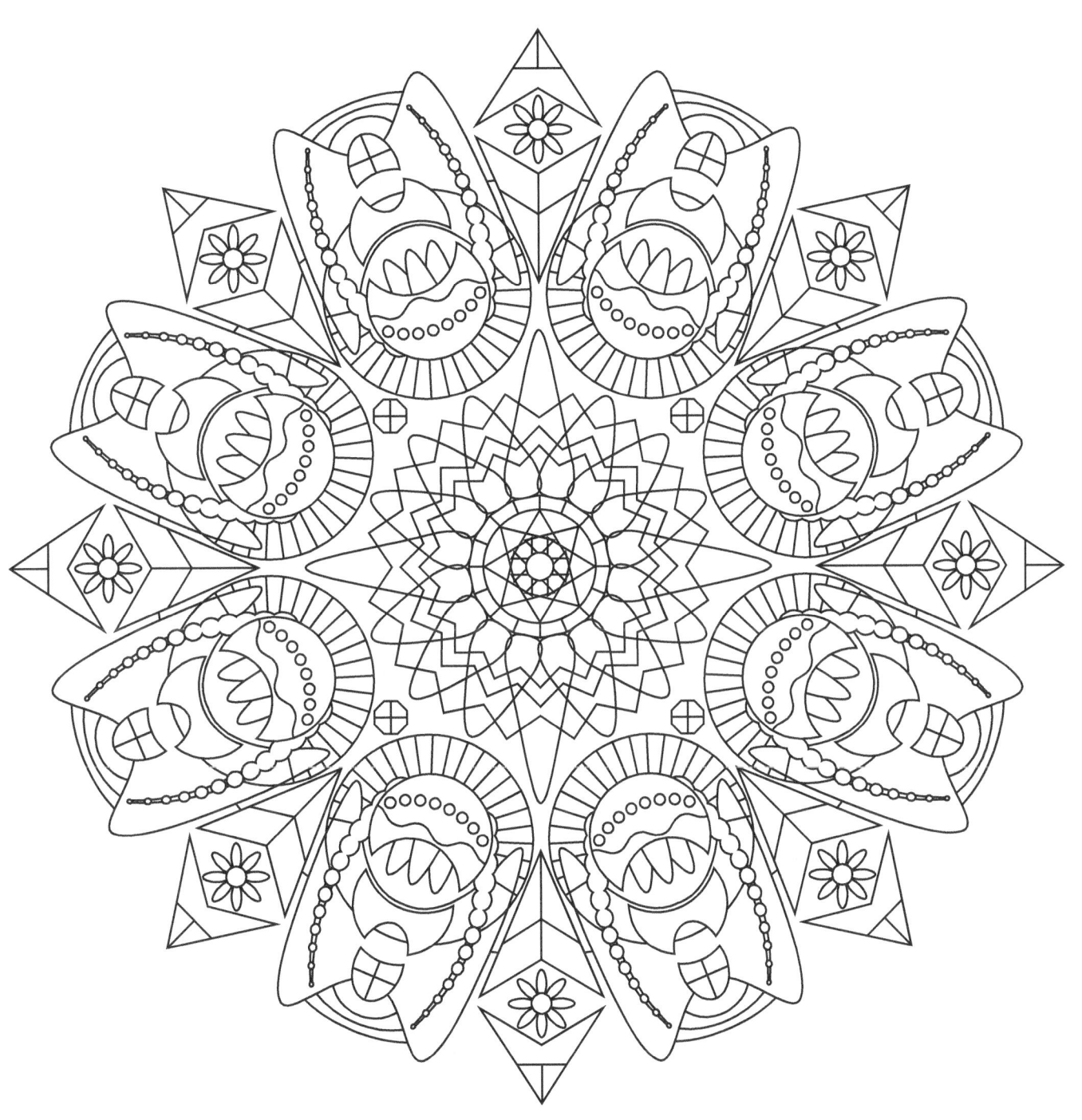

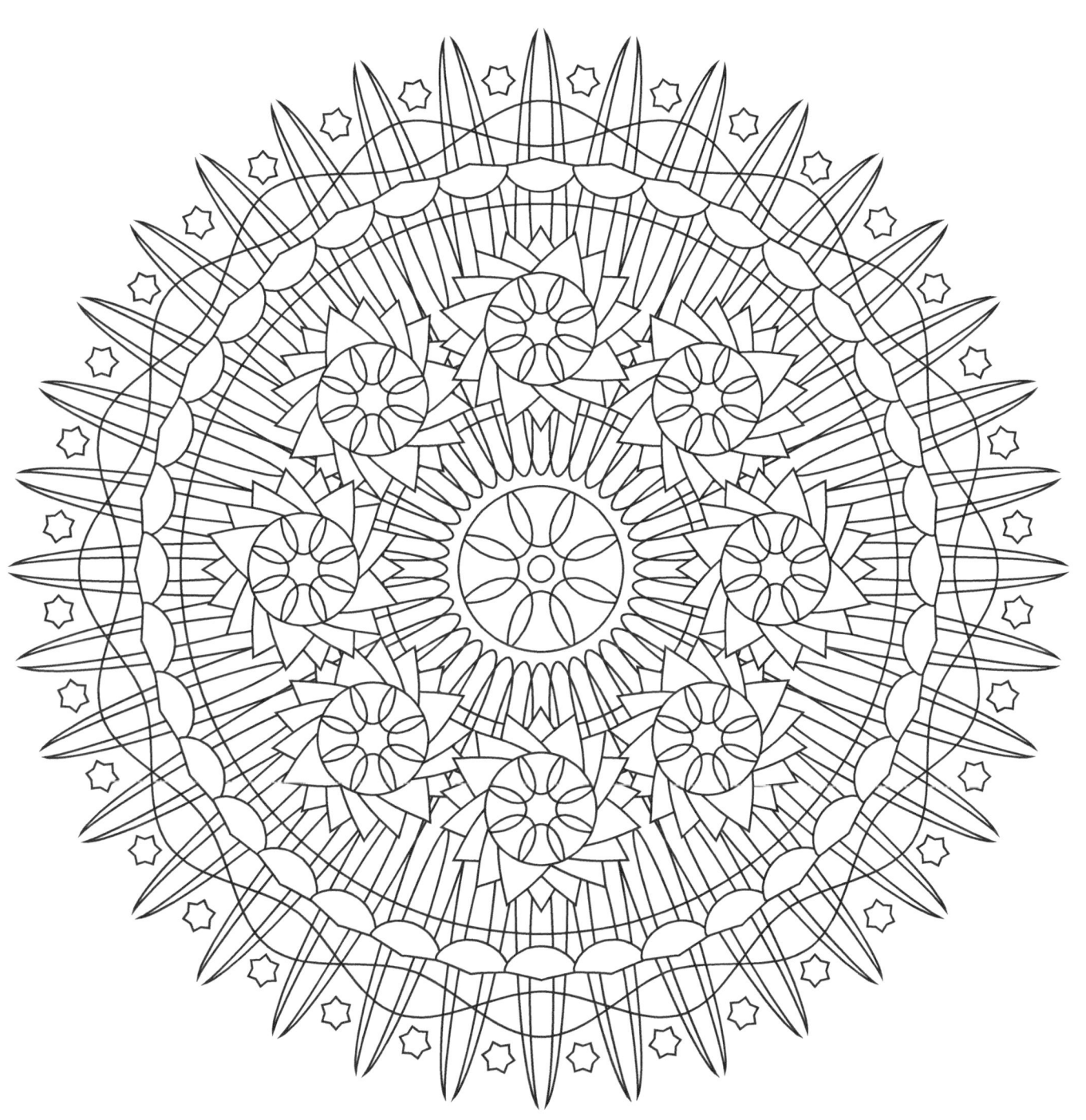

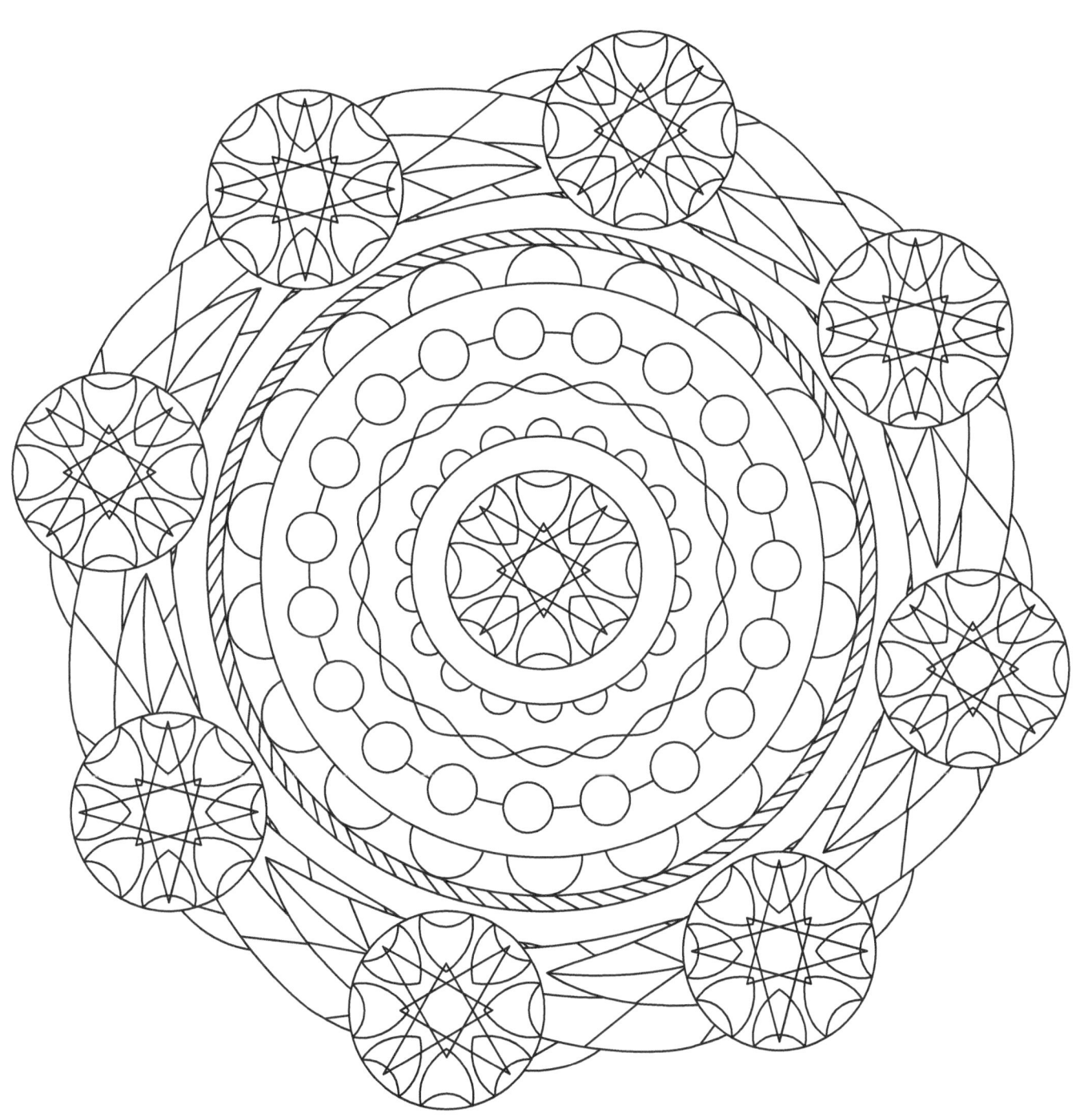

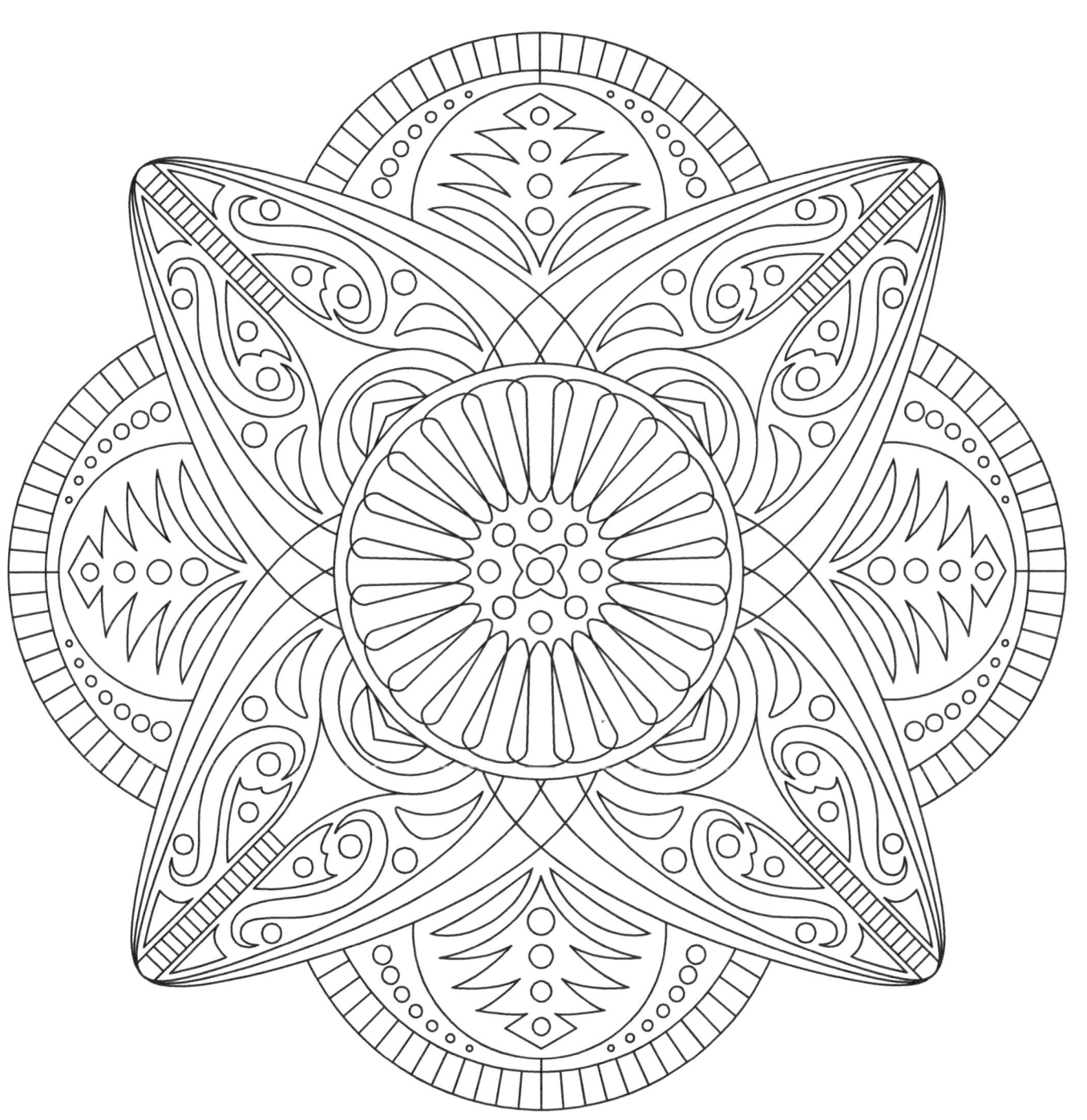

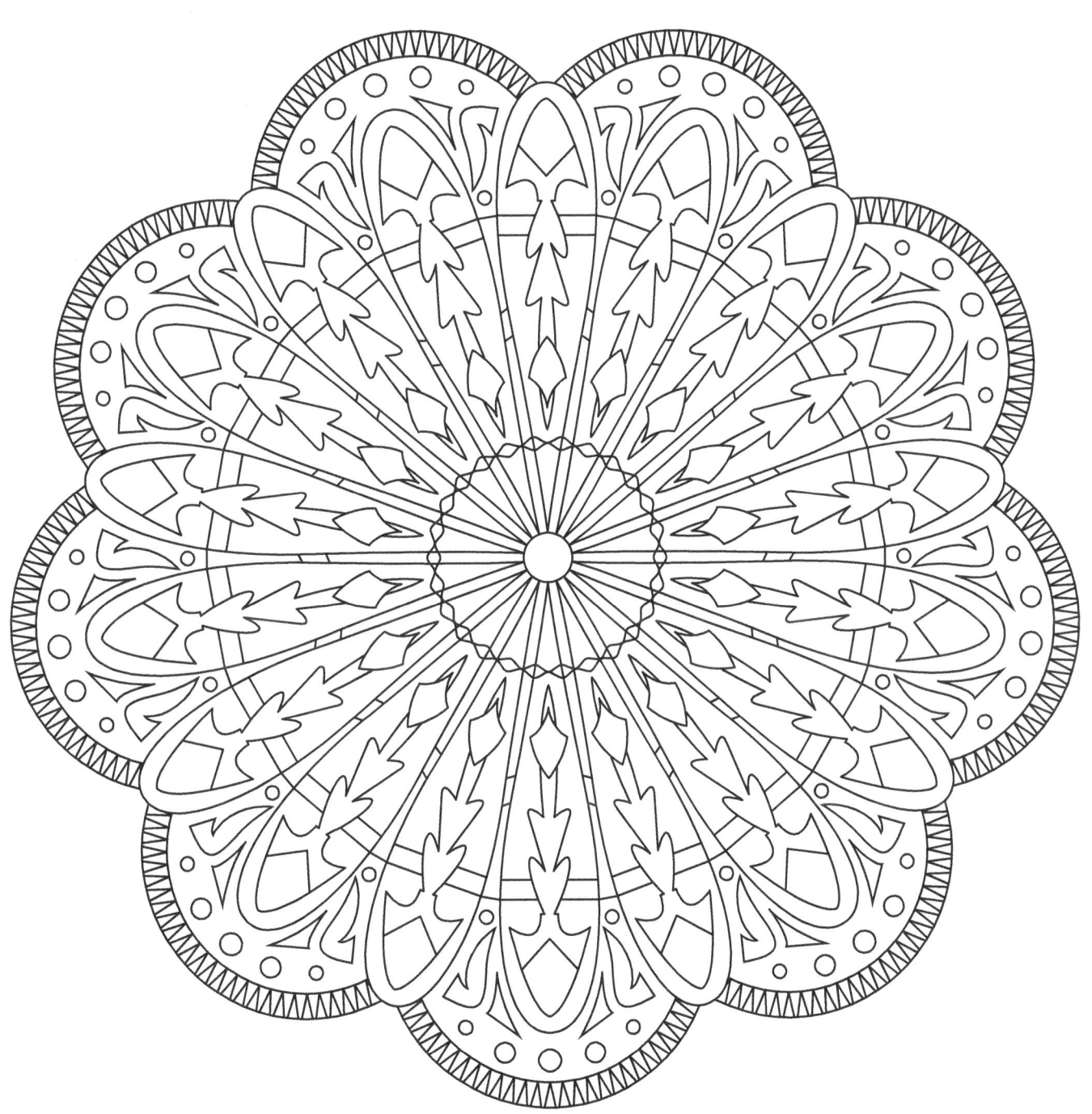

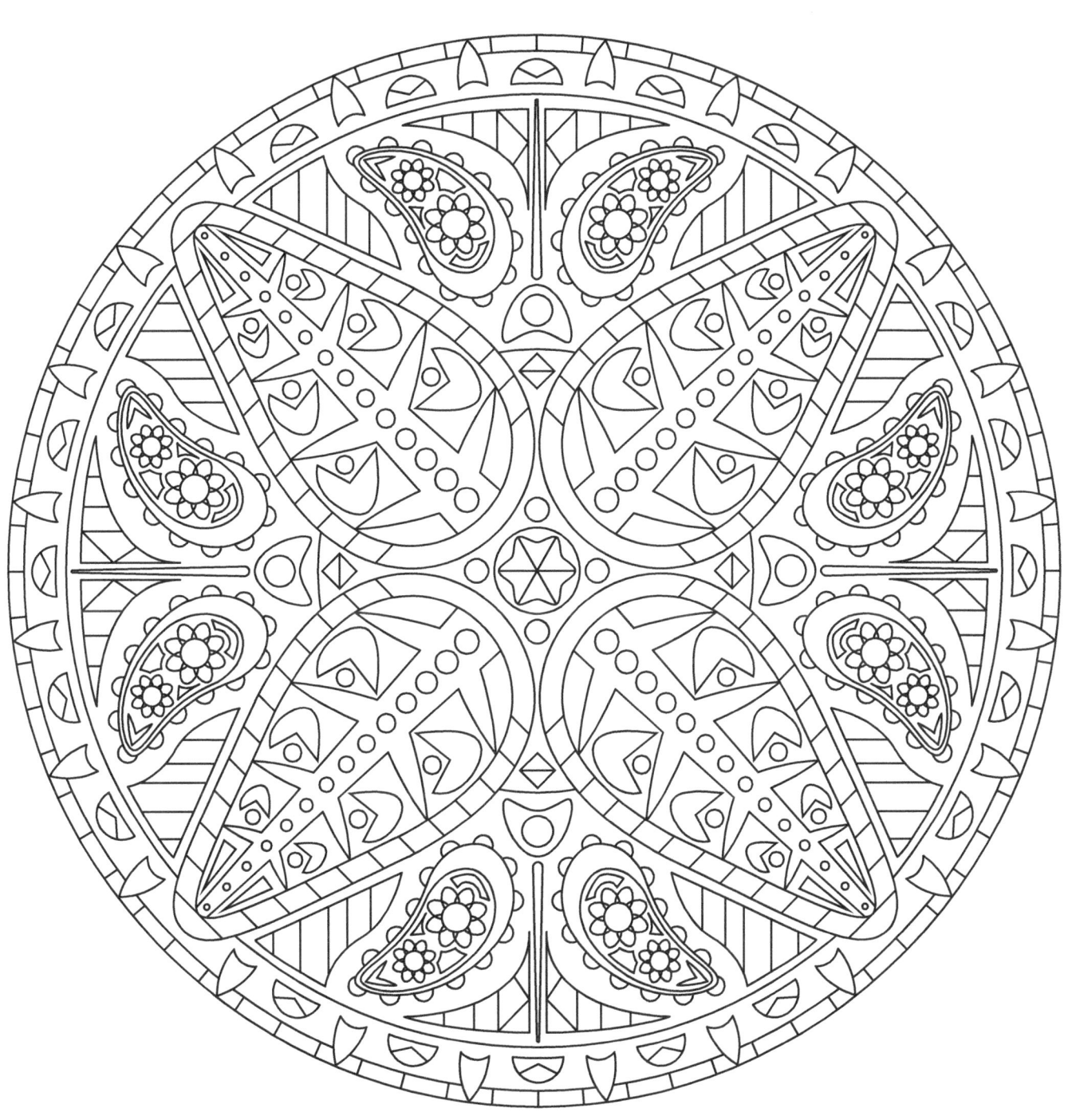

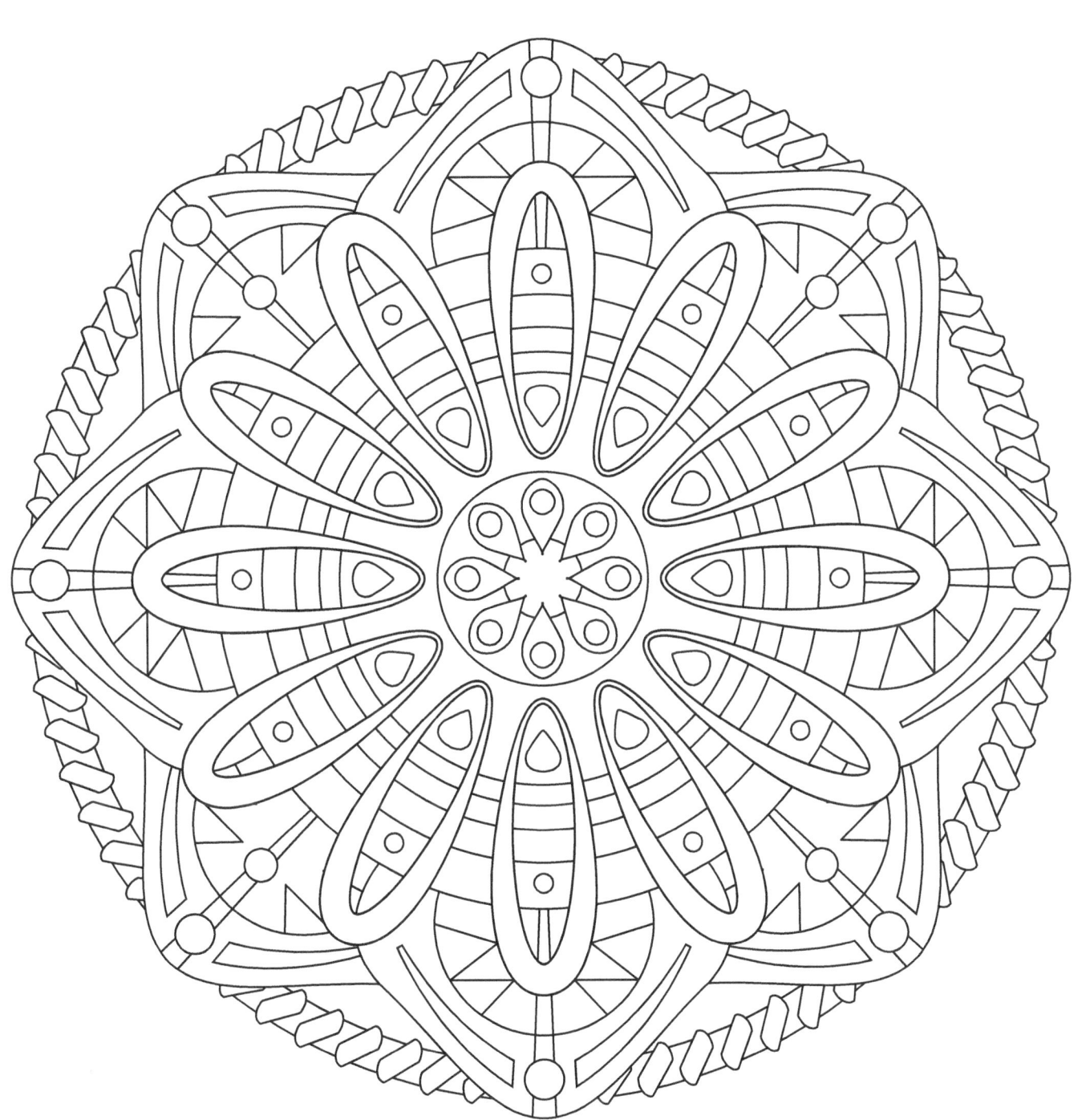